HORSE

HORSE

HOW THE HORSE HAS
SHAPED CIVILIZATIONS

J. Edward Chamberlin

ALFRED A. KNOPF CANADA

PUBLISHED BY ALFRED A. KNOPF CANADA

Copyright © 2006 J. Edward Chamberlin

www.randomhouse.ca

The images in the book are from Art Resource, New York, except for
Whistlejacket on page 195, which comes from the Bridgeman Art Library,
New York, and the photographs on pages 5, 55, and 270, which are by
Cynthia Dunne, and used with her kind permission.

Library and Archives Canada Cataloguing in Publication

Chamberlin, J. Edward, 1943–
Horse : how the horse has shaped civilization / J. Edward Chamberlin.
Includes index.

ISBN-13: 978-0-676-97868-1
ISBN-10: 0-676-97868-1

1. Horses—History. 2. Animals and civilization. I. Title.

SF283.C53 2006a   636.1009   C2006-901556-2

Text design: Cynthia Dunne

First Edition

Printed and bound in the United States of America

2 4 6 8 9 7 5 3 1

CONTENTS

OUT OF THE MIST

Horses and Humans in the Americas

It snowed every day from early December to late February, which was rare in the northern range of the Rockies; and the temperature went down to fifty below, which wasn't. The winter of 1932–33 had been the worst that anyone could remember. Anyone except Big Bird.

Big Bird was a horse, her name drawn from an Indian legend. A big gray mare, almost pure white by now, she knew the stories of the old, old days. She remembered one about a winter thousands of years before which went on so long that they forgot about everything but getting by. Back then, in a place where the ice hadn't covered the land, wondering whether winter would ever end, humans and horses first made friends.

The place looked different then. The forests hadn't yet covered the land, and the valleys hadn't been carved out as deeply. There were animals everywhere, wooly mammoths and grumpy rhinoceroses and large bears and small camels, swift antelope and toothy tigers, mean wolves and shaggy buffalo and sleek beaver and sly fox. You could see farther then, and the horses could run when the big cats and dogs—the tigers and the wolves—came after them. Everyone was watching everyone else to see what they were doing and whether they were having trouble and how long it would be before they would eat or be eaten. They were all holding on by the skin of their teeth.

Then some of the horses left, traveling over the tundra across the Bering Land Bridge, the doorway to Asia. At its most extensive, Beringia covered over five hundred miles from north to south, and stretched from central Siberia to the western Yukon. Even in the coldest times, it was free of ice except high in the hills, and it nourished a large number of animals. The horses who left spread across Asia; some carried on beyond the steppes to Europe, while others went south to India and Africa. But wherever they went, they traveled between the mountains and the rivers on the savannah lands.

Those horses that stayed behind in the Americas died out. Nobody quite knows why. They didn't die of the cold, because they survived worse in the places they went to. Maybe when the world became warmer they just wandered around as woodlands took over —like humans, horses are mostly at home on the range—and became easy prey. Maybe the shrubs and the grasses and the berries they ate became scarce. Maybe the humans, who must have been hard pressed to find enough food and were well outfitted with throwing sticks and fluted spear points, hunted them down. It doesn't take long, as we know from the prairie buffalo and the Atlantic cod. Perhaps other things happened.

Whatever the case, for at least ten thousand years, so it is said, there were no horses in the Americas. But eventually they came back home, suspended in slings in the Spanish caravels. And some say that they came earlier, cross-tied in the Viking longboats that ventured across the ocean.

☙

And they had all come back to *this*. Perhaps it was a big mistake. In the fall of 1932, Big Bird had heard the owls screaming, and had seen the crows shifting their wings sideways in flight. The fox and beaver pelts that the Indians trapped were heavier than usual. She had known it was going to be a bad winter. But this was the baddest of all. The snow had been very deep, forage had been terribly hard to find, and most of the horses had floundered and froze in the drifts.

The spring of '33 eventually came, blessing those who made it through. And out of the morning mist, suspended between the meadow and the mountain, came Big Bird, gaunt and gimpy. It was a big comedown for her. She prided herself on looking good and moving well—showing her bottoms, as farmers say when a horse picks up her feet nicely—and here she was, a bell around her neck and hobbles on her feet. She felt like a milk cow.

But once again, memory took over, and she remembered another time, around 50 million years ago, which she had heard the old ones tell about, when their earliest ancestor had appeared out of the morning mist way back at the beginning of time. Right around here, too. Dawn horse, she was called. Eohippus. *Small and short-legged, with toes (four on the front feet, and three on the back); teeth that were good for browsing leaves, but not tough enough for the sandpaper grasses; and a tippy-toe walk like a fox. They came on the scene when the dinosaurs died out, moving into*

*Horses have an extraordinary generosity of spirit, and
remarkable patience in dealing with humans.*

*a niche. It was the right move, for they did well, keeping company
with the other hippos.*

Eohippus *looked a lot like Eeyore, the donkey in* Winnie the
Pooh; *but instead of losing her tail, she lost her toes. At first, she
and her kin were at home in the rain forests and swamps, but as
these changed to savannah land all the places to hide disappeared,
replaced by places to run. So the toes went, slowly but surely, until
all that was left were some bones up above the ankle and a little bit
of the pad on the foot. The legs became longer, as* eohippus *changed
into* mesohippus *and* merychippus *and then* pliohippus, *running faster each time, rearing up higher, kicking harder, eventually
emerging from the evolutionary labyrinth as* equus.

When shrubs and bushes gave way to grasses and grains, their teeth changed, too, becoming high-crowned and cement-covered so that they could cut and grind rather than chomp and chew. Being easily surprised was their great strength back then, and Big Bird knew that it still was, watching and listening for predators, and smelling them. Their heads became bigger, the size of their eyes larger than those of even the largest mammals, the elephants and the whales, and more soulful, too; their ears rotated in all directions, and they developed a big nose to sniff out trouble, or another horse in heat. These horses were the legend of the Americas before anybody had legends. Before there was anybody.

≋

Mindy Christiansen heard Big Bird's bell first from across the creek. Then a kind of thumping, louder and louder. Then he saw the horses, seventeen of them, led by the old gray mare. Mares usually lead herds of horses—the Old English word for horse *was* "mearh"—while stallions come along behind to watch for trouble. There were no stallions left in this lot.

Big Bird's front feet were hobbled with a soft rope, its three strands unraveled, laid together parallel, the ends tied, looped around one pastern, twisted to set the length, and then slipped around the other pastern and twice through its strands. The other horses trailed behind with Bobby Attachie. He was from the *Dunne-za* band—Beaver Indians, Mindy called them. They were cousin to the Navajo and the Apache, as well as the Gwich'in and the Chipewyan north on the Mackenzie River, all speaking the same Athapaskan language. Bobby loved horses, and when he had time he would go into Fort St. John to ride in the rodeo. But this year there would be no time.

He lived in Peace River country, up near the Yukon on the way to Alaska, and named for a long-ago truce between two Indian tribes. There is a ridge up there, from which one can see the headwaters of three rivers, running in different directions to three great oceans: the Pacific, the Arctic, and the Atlantic. This was the place where humans and horses first met each other thousands of years earlier.

Mindy Christiansen, who was watching from the trail near where he had parked his truck, had been appointed Inspector of Indian Agencies for the region the previous spring. He knew a fair bit about horses, and a little bit about Indians. And he had heard about the terrible winter up there. But what he saw was worse than he expected. He made some notes to send to Ottawa:

7

June, 1933. There are 170 Indians in the band, belonging to the Beaver tribe. They are on their last legs. They have absolutely nothing. I have never seen a band of Indians who had less. During the two days I spent with them, it rained continually, and I noticed that these people did not even have tents. There were only two or three good teepees in the whole outfit and the only shelter they had was a piece of canvas hung over willows, under which I saw the old people and children huddled. They were very poorly clad and some of the children had practically nothing. They haven't even any cooking utensils. In February all of them took sick with bad colds. They've lived on moose meat since last summer; sometimes a little flour. No tea or tobacco. Two hundred horses died. . . .

≈

This was the time when the government in the United States was trying to deal with another disaster, one that wiped out many of the Indians, as well as their horses. It wasn't just one bad winter; it was fifty of them in a row, winters and summers too. In the late 1920s, the government had commissioned a report from the Institute for

Government Research (later known as the Brookings Institute) to address the devastation caused by the Dawes Act, which had been passed in 1887 to facilitate agricultural settlement on so-called idle land. It led to the dispossession of Indian territory, the destruction of Indian tribes, and the dislocation of Indian people. The report, directed by Lewis Meriam, was filled with well-researched indignation about the breaches of trust that had characterized Indian administration for a half century. It was harsh in its criticism of the allotment policy that had been put in place, and it recommended the reestablishment of tribal governments with control over land and resources. It was eloquent in its celebration of the values of community and of place, and the interdependence of spiritual and material values in both native and non-native society.

It was also incorrigibly utilitarian in the remedies it proposed. So when it came to describing the situation of the Navajo, one of the largest and most powerful of the tribes, it forgot about their horses. Actually, it didn't quite forget. It dismissed their horses in one paragraph in its nearly nine hundred pages. The paragraph was titled "Worthless Horses."

Worthless? These were the horses that worked the land, pulled the wagons, carried the men and women, and

9

herded the stock. They had hunted the buffalo on the northern plains, a staple of life and a sacred icon; they had given the Comanche and the Nez Perce and the Blackfoot and all the other peoples of the plains a new independence, and they had held everyone's imaginations, cowboys and Indians alike. For these were horses that grazed wild on the grasslands, defying the immediate demands of subsistence and signifying not just prestige but a kind of sovereignty. To the Navajo, a horse was not a convenience or a commodity but a covenant between fresh air and freedom to breath, a ceremony of belief in beauty and goodness.

All this completely confounded those who wrote the Meriam Report. They did not understand that horses were both useful and useless, and that that was why they were so important to the Navajo, who centuries before had traveled from the tundra and boreal forests of their Athapaskan kin to the drylands of the southwest. They were *Dene* people, which means the real people, and they met up with the Spaniards who were coming with their hacienda habits and their horses, and adopted both. The Navajo had seen horses before on their way down south, horses that had slipped away from the Spanish herds and become the legendary mustangs of the West. The Navajo

Navajo Chicken Fight (Tsireh Awa, ca. 1925–1930)

took to them, and like the plains peoples of Asia and Europe and Africa thousands of years before, they were never the same again.

Unlike many government reports, the Meriam Report was acted upon. The Indian Reorganization Act, landmark legislation under the New Deal, was passed at almost the same time that Mindy Christiansen was pondering the fate of those two hundred horses that died up in Peace River country. The Act was unquestionably on the progressive side of things, and called for the revitalization of local communities and the development of local economies. For the reform-minded officials working with the Navajo, this meant new grazing practices to reverse fifty years of abuse by white leaseholders and to sustain the sheep and the goats that were a staple of Navajo life. Accordingly, a livestock reduction program was proposed. It was based on what were called "sheep units." Everything was calculated in sheep units, especially worthless horses. On average, a horse ate as much grass there as five sheep; so horses were said to be the equivalent of five sheep. According to this calculus, the only good horse was a dead horse.

The Navajo had heard that one before. They also knew the state of their grasslands and the need for restrictions, having survived as a people for thousands of years, and for several hundreds in the drylands of the Southwest. But they refused to have their sense of who they were and where they belonged determined by a diminished, impoverished vision that saw everything reducible to sheep units. The Indian agent with the Navajo at the time, Reeseman Fryer, said later that he thought that single phrase—sheep units—inflicted a deeper wound on the Navajo than almost anything else in those times of suffering and sacrifice. The federal government directed the Navajo to round up their five-sheep-unit horses, and sell or destroy them. The Navajo said no.

The refusal of the Navajo to embrace the livestock reduction program and its sheep units had to do with more than just horses. But horses were at the heart of it, representing Navajo resistance to those who deemed horses nothing more than a worthless indulgence, an offense against the social utility and economic morality of the American New Deal.

The reasons for this standoff—and for many similar ones—are often laid at the door of ignorant officials. If only those responsible for introducing these changes had known more about the Navajo, or about tribal governments, or about land management, or about horses. But in fact they *did* know a great deal about all of these. They knew the Navajo, and Navajo country. The man most responsible for the initiatives that led to the restoration of tribal government and the land conservation program and those pernicious sheep units was John Collier, who became Commissioner of Indian Affairs in the 1930s and implemented the Meriam Report. He was an eloquent social activist who had taught at the People's Institute in

New York, lived among the Pueblo, and was deeply committed to self-determination for native peoples and respect for the diversity of their cultures.

Therefore he should have known better. He should have known about horses being important to people in ways that go well beyond everyday utility. He had read widely, and he had listened to Navajo stories about horses and heroes and the knowledge they provided of how to keep the everyday at bay.

But he had forgotten about the stories he knew best, the ones he really believed in. In the Program of Great Books that he helped develop through the New York Public Library and the People's Institute and eventually Columbia University and liberal arts programs across the country, there were a lot of stories about horses. The list of Great Books included Chinese classics that celebrated the "heavenly horses of Ferghana," and told of how the first emperor of the Qin dynasty built a great mausoleum underground, with terra-cotta figures of soldiers and chariots and over six hundred life-size horses. There were Persian poems about special horses with the leopard and snow blanket spots of the Appaloosas, and the medieval *Morte d'Arthur*, in which chivalry—from the French

word for horse, *cheval*—came into its own. And there was
the Qur'an, in which rules for breeding and training
horses were revealed, and it was said that for every barley
corn that is given to a horse, Allah will pardon one sin.
When he died and went to heaven, Muhammad rode a
horse.

And there was another story among those Great
Books, one of the classics of Western literature. After the
siege and sacking of the city of Troy, the Greek hero
Achilles drags the corpse of the Trojan commander
Hector in the dust behind his horses to the funeral pyre of
his friend Patroclus, whom Hector had killed. Then he
leaves Hector there in the open to be eaten by dogs and
birds. But other powers are at work to maintain some ceremony. The goddess Aphrodite anoints Hector's body
with ambrosia, and Apollo keeps the sun away to save it
from rotting, until finally on Zeus's command—and the
payment of a large ransom—Achilles delivers up the body
to Hector's father.

"Thus held they funeral for Hector, tamer of horses."
These are the final words of Homer's epic *Iliad*, a story
from the crossroads of Europe and Asia and Africa, and
they hold out a promise of dignity in the face of defeat

and death. Not "Hector, worth five hundred sheep-units," but "Hector, tamer of horses."

⤙⤙

Oh, but that all happened such a long time ago, one might say. And such a long way off. But of course it didn't. Hector was Bobby Attachie, walking down the valley with Big Bird and the others as they came out of the mist and into their own history. Bobby knew all about the value of horses. Down the road in Fort St. John, it cost twice as much to stable your horse as it did to get a bed in the local hotel (. . . not that he had ever done either). He knew how horses, like humans, could be both worthless and priceless.

But right now none of that mattered to Bobby. Like Hector, tamer of horses, he just wanted to make sure that Big Bird and the others survived into the summer.

His horses didn't like those hobbles—Big Bird especially. But they hadn't eaten anything much for days, with the washouts and the winterkill, and she knew that Bobby had put the hobbles on to make sure she didn't take the others too far into the valley where they would eat fresh grass and get a stomachache. Horses are amazingly strong, but a simple stomachache can do them in. It's called colic, in horses as in humans; but horses die from it, more than from any other single disease.

The history of horses begins with digestion and indigestion. All too often, it ends there too. Their stomachs are small, relative to their size, and like most of us they become uncomfortable when they are empty. So although they don't eat a lot at any one time, they eat almost constantly if they can. That's why we talk about eating like a horse.

Horses have a strong digestive system, and can handle almost everything from bark and berries to nuts and leaves. But they also have a strange digestive system, in which their breathing and their eating are combined. It makes it impossible for them to vomit.

So unlike cows, which are able to bring back undigested food in wads or "cuds," horses only get one chance. They nibble, chew, swallow, and digest. Or indigest. That's when the trouble starts. Indigestion is serious business for a horse. Overeating can cause it, or drinking too much after a workout; a long spell out in cold weather can bring it on, or a sudden change in rations (especially after a winter like the 1932–33 one), or worms. Poisonous plants are particularly dangerous—in the country where Big Bird lived, larkspur and locoweed

and lupines and some species of camass were deadly—
and other poisons too, the mysterious ones that you hear
about around a racetrack. And all because horses can't
throw up.

The treatment for horse colic is common across cultures. Find a way to release gas from the stomach by
puncturing it or putting in a tube from either end; or
neutralize the poisons by forcing medicine down the
throat. Boiled plants such as turnip and snake weed and
carrotleaf and bitterroot were common among the plains
Indians, while a powder made from dried snake skin dis-
solved in water was—and still is—used by the Kazaks on
the Eurasian steppes. The rest of us try mineral oil, or various other concoctions known only to the local veteri-
narian (or the fellow down the road).

Bobby Attachie wasn't planning to lose any horses
from colic, and certainly not Big Bird. She was an easy
keeper, but she was special, with ancestors raised in
another valley, in the region called La Perche in France,
where Percherons were bred. That was the country where
people had once painted horses on the walls of caves deep
in the ground, and where heavy horses were used by
knights at the time of Charlemagne. They were later

A painting in the Lascaux caves in France

crossed with breeds from northern Europe and Africa, especially Norman and Arab stock, to produce one of the great draft horses of the world—the Percheron. They were brought to the Americas in the nineteenth century, where they quickly became popular, while back in France, in the 1880s, 15,000 of them pulled the carriages of the Paris Omnibus Company. For all their size and strength, they have a grace of movement that is rare in a heavy horse.

Big Bird had all that and more, for on the other side her family was from Andalusia, in Spain. The Andalusians were originally a cross between Barbs—the Bedouin horses from the Barbary Coast—and the Arab horses that trace their lineage back to Ishmael, son of Abraham, another legendary tamer of horses.

If humans danced before they walked, as the eighteenth-century scholar Giambattista Vico said, Andalusians were probably as close to human as a horse gets. They became famous for their moves in the formal arenas of *haute école*, or high school for horses, and they founded many other breeds, such as the Lippizaner (the horse of the 250-year-old Spanish Riding School in Vienna), the Kladruber (from one of the oldest breeding stables—or "studs," as they are called—in Europe, founded in 1579 in Bohemia by Emperor Rudolf II), and the Lusitano (the legendary Portuguese bull-fighting horse). The Andalusians came across to the Americas with the Spanish; and the Quarter Horse, the Mustang, the Appaloosa, and the Argentinean Criollo all have Andalusian ancestors.

The Spaniards weren't the only ones who had brought their horses along. Mindy Christiansen's uncle had brought Fjord horses from Norway when he came to the Americas in the 1880s. They were small, with long choppers and big rumps and a dun-colored coat that is ancient, and they could survive when almost nothing else could. Their ancestors were the Tarpans of the western Russian steppes, favored for their meat and hunted out of existence by the nineteenth century. Fjord horses were some of the first to pull a plow. The Vikings rode them, and when the Normans invaded England in 1066 they used the knowledge of their Norwegian ancestors to bring horses across the Channel—10 to a boat, 350 boats in all. And so it was on horseback, with archers riding in what were then revolutionary stirrups, that they defeated Harold at the Battle of Hastings and altered the course of European history.

When the Fjord horses and the Andalusian horses and the Arabs and the Percherons came to the Americas, they were returning home to where horses really came from. And they met up with those who called themselves the real people of the Americas, the *Dunne-za* and the *Sao-kitapiikse* of the northern plains. The Blackfoot.

Together, they remembered those ancient horses heading west across the land bridge, while eastward through the mist came peo-ple, bolder than the horses but no less bewildered. As they passed each other, the horses going one way and the humans another, they must have wondered who was going in the wrong direction. "Good luck," they shouted to each other. "Turn left, or maybe right if you feel lucky, when you get to the big river." Then each went their separate ways, melting into history.

Thousands of years later, they met each other again. The horses had circled the world, and grown up. The humans had covered the whole continent, and become the great aboriginal cultures of the Americas. They took to the horses, and the horses took to them, and they both changed.

In the nineteenth century, the Blackfoot confederacy of the northern plains included the Blood tribe (they called themselves *Kainai*), the Piegan (or *Aapatohsipiikani*), and the *Siksika*. Together, they had become one of the great horse cultures of the world, and all in a remarkably short time. It was just 150 years since the Blackfoot had gone to war against the Shoshone, so the tribal historians said, down in what is now Idaho and Utah, and had seen big horses in battle. They were badly beaten, and from then on, they knew that they needed horses. They first got them from the Nez Perce.

There were of course stories among the Blackfoot about where horses *really* came from, just as we all have stories about the things that are most important to us. Creation stories, the stories of science, his stories and her stories. They each have their place in our lives, and many of us believe them all. One of these Blackfoot myths of the origin of horses was written down in the 1880s:

A long time ago there was a poor boy who tried to obtain secret power so that he might be able to get some of the things he wanted but did not have. He went out from his camp and slept alone on the mountains, near great rocks, beside rivers. He wandered until he came to a large lake northeast of the Sweetgrass Hills. By the side of that lake he broke down and cried. The powerful water spirit—an old man—who lived in that lake heard him and told his son to go to the boy and find out why he was crying. The son went to the sorrowing boy and told him that his father wished to see him. "But how can I go to him?" the lad asked. "Hold onto my shoulders and close your eyes," the son replied. "Don't look until I tell you to do so." They started into the water. As they moved along the son told the boy, "My father will offer you your choice of animals in this lake. Be sure to choose the old mallard and its little ones."

When they reached his father's lodge on the bottom of the lake, the son told the boy to open his eyes. They entered the lodge, and the old man said, "Come sit over here." Then he asked, "My boy, what did you come for?" The boy explained, "I have been a very poor boy. I left my camp to look for secret power so that I may be able to start out for myself." The old man then said, "Now, son, you are going to become the leader of your tribe. You will have plenty of everything. Do you see all the animals in this lake? They are all mine." The boy, remembering the son's advice, said, "I should thank you for giving me as many of them as you can." Then the old man offered him his choice. The boy asked for the mallard and its young. The old man replied, "Don't take that one. It is old and of no value." But the boy insisted. Four times he asked for the mallard. Then the old man said, "You are a wise boy. When you leave my lodge my son will take you to the edge of the lake, and there, in the darkness, he will catch the mallard for you. When you leave the lake don't look back."

The boy did as he was told. At the edge of the lake the water spirit's son collected some marsh grass and braided it into a rope. With the rope he caught the old mallard and led it ashore. He placed the rope in the boy's hand and told him to walk on, but not to look back until daybreak. As the boy walked along he heard the duck's feathers flapping on the ground. Later he could no longer hear that sound. As he proceeded he heard the sound of heavy feet behind him, and a strange noise, the cry of an animal. The braided marsh grass turned into a rawhide rope in his hand. But he did not look back until dawn.

At daybreak he turned and saw a strange animal at the end of the line—a horse. He mounted it and, using the rawhide rope as a bridle, rode back to camp. Then he found that many horses had followed him.

The people of the camp were afraid of the strange animals. But the boy signed to them not to fear. He dismounted and tied a knot in the tail of his horse. Then he gave everybody horses; there were plenty for everyone and he had quite a herd left over for himself. Five of the older men in camp gave their daughters to him in return for the horses. They gave him a fine lodge also.

Until that time the people had had only dogs. But the boy told them how to handle the strange horses. He showed them how to use them for packing, how to break them for riding and for the travois, and he gave the horse its name, elk dog. One day the men asked him, "These elk dogs, would they be of any use in hunting buffalo?" "They are fine for that," the boy replied. "Let me show you." Whereupon he taught his people how to chase the buffalo on horseback. He also showed them how to make whips and other gear for their horses. Once when they came to a river the boy's friends asked him, "These elk dogs, are they of any use to us in the water?" He replied, "That is where they are best. I got them from the water." So they learned how to use horses in crossing streams.

The boy grew older and became a great chief, the leader of his people. Since that time every chief has owned a lot of horses.

Bobby Attachie had heard that story on a trip south, and that's why he named his gray mare Big Bird.

❧

Back in the 1880s, the world was much different. But winter was winter, and it had been a hard one. The weather was cold, though it was drier than during Big Bird's winter of hardship, with only a foot of snow covering the grass. The horses and cattle had to scrape and scuffle their way through.

When there wasn't enough to graze on, the Blackfoot horses would turn to browsing, as their ancestors had, and eat the bark of the cottonwood trees growing by the creek beds. Some elders said that cottonwood bark was better than oats. Nobody asked the horses, but they ate it. On a good day, horses need to eat about two percent of their body weight; for an average size horse that is about twenty pounds. Rustling up food is a full-time job for a horse.

And horses need to drink, up to ten gallons a day. Green grass provides a fair amount of that in spring and summer, but in the winter it's nowhere near enough. And water is often hard to find. But horses have special gifts when it comes to water. Where it is hidden in waterholes, as it is in many parts of the world, they will paw at the ground to show the place. Horses are diviners, water witchers, seekers of the sources of life. And when they find water, they draw it in like a suction pump, filling up faster than a racing car. That can get them into trouble if they are hot and bothered, or have been eating lots of grain.

Horses are able to go for a good while with less; in fact, some of the horses of the Mongols were famous for going days without food and water. These Blackfoot horses were tough, but not that tough. What they *were* is stoic—all horses are. Unlike humans, they seldom complain. Whinging and whining are for predators, like dogs and cats who howl and yowl at the smallest inconvenience. When you are prey, as horses have always been, you keep quiet. A sign of weakness is a sentence of death.

The Blackfoot had several stories about where horses came from. The one about the old mallard; and one about the Shoshone and the Nez Perce, who rode horses before they ever met a white man. And another, even older one, about how horses came out of the water and lived among them in the days after the ice melted and before the land dried up. But those horses were small, no bigger than a fox or a rabbit, too small for riding or packing, and anyway

Horse effigy used as war medicine by the Blackfoot

they used dogs back then. The stories that scientists tell about horses are just as full of contradictions, and like the Blackfoot ones, they don't always agree with each other.

Wolves and dogs first taught the Blackfoot how to hunt, in packs. You can still see them in the sky as *makoi-yohsokoyi,* the Wolf Trail or Milky Way, reminding the people how to work together. The wolves also told them that animals with hoofs and horns were alright to eat, but those with paws and claws should be left alone. Horses were never keen on this, but when the Blackfoot got the big horses and called them *ponokaomitai-ksi,* or elk-dogs, the horses liked that name, and felt honored when elk antlers were used in sacred rituals.

Horse medicine (*ponokaomitai saam*) was the most powerful medicine among the Blackfoot, and the Horse Dance its central ceremony, through which humans as well as horses were brought back to health with medicines that included wild peony, baneberry, and sagebrush. The Blackfoot had sayings about horses which helped them live their lives and face death. And just as Muhammad rode to heaven, their great leaders returned to the spirit world with their favorite horses.

By the early nineteenth century, the Blackfoot had

developed extraordinary skills in horsemanship. They had saddles and bridles and all sorts of other horse tack richly woven and worked for both war and peace and the ceremonies of each that had become part of their culture; and they had over a hundred words for the different colors of horses. The Kazaks in central Asia, still one of the great horse cultures of the world, have a color scheme that is even more exact; they have sixty-two words for bay shades alone. In fact, though we are not so good on colors, we aren't shy of strange and subtle words in English when it comes to the parts of a horse's body, like poll, throatlatch, cannon, fetlock, chestnut, croup, dock, stifle, gaskin, hock, pastern, and coronet.

And the Blackfoot had stories and songs about horses, Black Beauty stories—they even made rocking horses for their children—and Seabiscuit stories, for they loved horse racing, and a good racehorse was highly prized.

My grandfather John Cowdry moved to Blackfoot territory in southern Alberta in the 1880s, and there he befriended Crop Eared Wolf, a *Kainai*.

Crop Eared Wolf liked fast horses, ones with high withers (where the neck, shoulder, and back of a horse meet) for comfort on long rides, and a long, low, flat croup (the topline from the loin, at the end of the back, to the base of the tail) for endurance, and that shade of blue-gray the cowboys called grulla. Horses of that color, he said, were tougher than the rest, bearing up in the brutal cold and heat of the northern plains. The Arabs, living in the desert, liked grays too, especially those the color of the wild pigeon.

But what Crop Eared Wolf really loved was stealing horses. And he was very, very good at it, legendary among his people and loathed by others. Sometimes he thought of himself as liberating the horses from a hard life with the Sioux or the Shoshone. Other times, he thought of how powerful he would be with plenty of horses. Many Horses, a great chief before him who liked pintos—or paints, as they were often called—had over five hundred horses.

Crop Eared Wolf had just come back from a raid all the way down to the Yellowstone River, where he stole forty horses from the Flathead and the Crow. But these were changing times. The border between Canada and the United States was being surveyed, and his adventure caused an international incident. Also, the North West Mounted Police had arrived in Blackfoot territory just ten years earlier, having ridden west to establish a presence in the country that had only just become Canada, and to help make treaties with the Indians. They were also there for the coming of the railroad. The iron horse. Along with the telegram and the telephone, and soon the car and the truck, the train offered new forms of transportation and communication that would transform the world. Just as the horses had done long before.

The Mounties, who built stables for their horses before they built barracks for their men, weren't happy about horse-stealing. It kept alive old quarrels and started new ones. Also, they stood to lose by it themselves, for even the forts they built were no defense against the likes of Crop Eared Wolf, known to have stolen prize horses from enemy camps at night, while their reins were attached to a chief's wrist as he slept in his teepee.

Crop Eared Wolf wanted to hold on to the old ways, at least when it came to horses. Horses made him feel human. More than human. When he rode horses, or watched them running, he felt the spirit alive in him. *Whose* spirit, he couldn't say. But he could say that there was a moment when he felt one with both the earth and the sky. "Airs above ground," they called the amazing moves of the Lippizaner, like the *capriole*. "Drinking the wind," the Arabs said. "Horse medicine," Crop Eared Wolf called it.

But he understood that some things must change, for the buffalo were almost gone. An elder who kept a record of each year on a buffalo hide—what the Blackfoot called a buffalo count—had described the year before last as "when first there were no buffalo." Crop Eared Wolf had heard how the great buffalo-hunting Metis on the central plains, led by Louis Riel and Gabriel Dumont, had made a last stand against the agricultural settlement of the region. Louis Riel was hanged for treason. Gabriel Dumont joined Buffalo Bill's Wild West Show.

Suddenly, the Blackfoot seemed to be losing a way of life that had originally been created by horses and humans thousands of years earlier, when their ancient kin—the tribes of central Asia—had first ridden a horse and spread out across the steppes in nomadic civilizations that became a wonder of the world. The Blackfoot and the other plains Indian tribes were the custodians of this way of life in the Americas.

In the beginning, the horses were the ones hunted for meat and hide and hair and hoof and bone. But eventually, horses offered a new way to hunt *other* animals, animals like the buffalo, *iiniiksi* in Blackfoot. Buffalo soon gave the Blackfoot everything they needed by way of food and shelter, clothing to keep them warm in the coldest weather, all sorts of tools and glues and threads, and skins to write on and rattles to dance with. Before horses, the Blackfoot followed the buffalo on foot and crept up on them downwind or surprised them from behind a bluff and speared them or shot them with bows and arrows or chased them along prairie driveways marked with stones and shrubs and sticks draped with coyote or wolf hides and ran them over natural rock outcrops, called buffalo jumps, where those who survived the fall would be quickly killed by men with clubs and spears.

This was what hunters seem to have done for thousands

Buffalo Chase with Bows and Lances (George Catlin, 1832–33)

of years, even hunting horses this way. Some of the cave paintings in Europe, over 15,000 years old, show marks to represent drive lanes and corrals. At Solutré, in east-central France, archeologists have found the bones of 100,000 horses in an area just a few hundred yards wide, in the lee of a limestone ridge. They were killed in communal hunts during a long period beginning about 35,000 years ago. Some say the hunters drove the horses over the bluff, like the Blackfoot did with the buffalo.

Horses don't believe a word of it. They never ran together in big bunches like that, they insist, and when they are frightened—which is quite often—they flee in single file, or break off in different directions. Horses are smarter than buffalo, they will remind you. And remember, Big Bird might add, the name of the great buffalo jump down in southern Alberta. It's called Head-Smashed-In Buffalo Jump. But the head wasn't the head of a horse, or even a buffalo. It was some silly young man who got in the way.

❧

Virginia Woolf once said that "on or about December 1910, human character changed." She was referring to the Post-impressionist exhibition at the Grafton Gallery in London, which ran from November 8, 1910, to January 15, 1911, and introduced new forms of truth-telling in painting. But she might well have been referring to the moment when horses began to be replaced by machines for getting around and sending messages, for hauling loads and helping on the farm, for waging war and showing off. When Indians lost their land as a consequence of the Dawes Act, selling it to settlers and speculators, the first thing many of them bought was a car.

In the fifty years between Crop Eared Wolf and John Cowdry in the 1880s and Bobby Attachie and Mindy Christiansen in the 1930s, a lot had happened. More than the habit of horse-stealing had changed—the whole world had changed. Not in the way it did fifty million years ago—when eohippus first appeared in the Americas in the dawn of time; or fifteen thousand—when humans hunted horses, and painted them on the walls of their caves; or five thousand—when horses began to be part of the human family, and were first driven and ridden; or even five hundred years ago—when they came back to the Americas. But the change was no less dramatic.

By the time Mindy Christiansen met Bobby Attachie, telephones and radios and cars and trucks had arrived, and airplanes were taking off. In the spring of 1933, the last thing anyone needed was worthless horses.

A year later, the Director of Indian Affairs came from Ottawa on a tour of the western reserves. His name was Harold McGill, and Christiansen brought him to see Bobby Attachie and the Indians at Fort St. John. He couldn't believe what had happened in such a short time, and he wanted McGill to see for himself. This is how McGill described the visit:

> It is one of the finest reserves I have seen. The south-west corner is covered with heavy timber and bush, a small river runs through the centre of the reserve, which covers 18,000 acres, and the gently sloping sides of the valley present a large area of good arable land. At the time of my visit, the pea-vine and vetches reached to my knees, and there was an abundance of ripe Saskatoon berries. The band to whom it belongs is composed of hunting and fishing Indians who do not live there, but use it for a camping ground in the summer.
>
> I walked across from the end of the road for two or three miles until we found the Indian encampment well concealed in a glade near a creek. These are the

Indians regarding whom Mr. Christiansen reported so graphically a year ago. There were a couple of dozen tents and teepees in the encampment. The dogs were less clamorous with their barking than is usually the case in an Indian camp. There was an abundance of moose meat drying on stages and rack, and a large quantity of Saskatoon berries were spread out on canvas to dry in the sun, after which they will be pounded into the dried moose meat to make pemmican. The tents that we visited were well supplied with moose meat and other varieties of food such as sugar, flour and tea. They appeared well fed and happy. Their horses were wellnourished.

A short year after Big Bird had come hip-hopping along, a bell around her neck, they had built back their herd to over a hundred horses. Wellnourished horses.

C h a p t e r   2

BRINGING HORSES HOME

Hunting Horses, Farming Horses

As early as 35,000 years ago, in caves that were their temples and shrines and sometimes their living rooms and bedrooms, people "papered" the walls with exquisite paintings and engravings—incisions, actually—of horses running up and down and across, in company with rhinoceroses and lions and bisons and bears and—in the Chauvet cave in what is now southeastern France—a big bird. At Chauvet, the paintings are nearly twice as old as those at the better-known caves of Lascaux, Niaux, and Pech Merle, and considerably older than those at Cosquer and Cougnac; but together with these and other cave paintings throughout the world they have transformed our understanding of ancient art and life, confirming a widespread tradition of representation and stylization going back to Stone Age times.

This is the early history of humanity, and horses are consistently present. The tradition includes carvings in ivory all across Europe and Asia; decorative pendants representing horses' heads, often made from the bone in a horse's tongue; and tools such as shaft-straighteners and spear-throwers with horse images on them. Along with the cave paintings, these celebrate the spectacular importance of horses—running free in the fields of the imagination—to people who defied the soulless utilitarians of ancient times.

And there would have been some of those; there always are. These were *very* hard times, in which hard facts were foremost: horses were hunted for food and hides, and humans were holding on with tools and techniques that seem primitive to us. But together, horses and humans created one of our most enduring legacies of art and craft.

A horse painting in the Lascaux caves

It may have taken thousands of years for horses to be valued for their strength and their speed more than for their flesh and their hide; but from the beginning they were valued for their spirit, as these Paleolithic paintings and carvings demonstrate. The paintings in particular celebrate not only the grace and beauty of horses, but their presence, a presence that haunted the imagination long after the herd had come and gone, the horses been captured or killed, the stories told and forgotten. And we can be sure we have so far seen only a small fraction of what was produced tens of thousands of years ago; the Chauvet cave was just discovered—or rediscovered—in the 1990s.

Some say these paintings represented the dreams of shamans, a vision of imagined horses rather than an imitation of real ones. They may have been, and if so, they must have been part of a truly extraordinary tradition of visual representation. But they were also a wake-up call to hunters, a reminder of the presence of something that wasn't right there—the horses which they were going out to hunt—and which they had to meet up with in their minds before they could catch up with them on those Eurasian moors. This is the essence of magic, of memory, and of all forms of art. It is also the basis of hunting and tracking.

The one thing hunters know when they see a track is that the animal isn't there. And they know that's all they know. This fact is at the heart of hunting and tracking, and it is at the heart of all forms of representation.

Representation in words and images is as old as humankind. We often say that our modern civilization began with reading, and with the new reading practices that emerged during the late Middle Ages and the Renaissance as print technology created a world on paper, a world of things that we could read about, a form of visual representation in which the word is both the thing and not the thing. "Horse" is not a horse. It is the word for a horse.

But the reading practices that developed in medieval and modern Europe were in fact flourishing 30,000 years ago in the highly sophisticated reading traditions of hunting societies around the world and in the paintings, sculptures, and other representations they made of animals. They had an understanding of the contradictions of representation that was as complex as ours, and in their magic charms and mysterious riddles as well as in their cave murals and carvings, they were reminding each other that a horse could be both there and not there all at the same time.

Paleolithic painters were our first modern artists. Our first postmodern artists too, for they loved playing with the relationships between reality and the imagination. "It was, and it was not," is how the storytellers of Majorca begin their stories. "They are and they are not," the cave painters reply across the millennia, referring to their horses. Among the herders and hunters of southern Namibia and the Kalahari, the word "|garube" is used to start a story ("|" indicates a soft click made at the front of the mouth); it means "the happening that is not happening." The novelist E. L. Doctorow was once criticized for bringing characters together in his historical novel

Ragtime who could not possibly have met in real life. "They have now," he replied.

It was in such contradictions that cave paintings became art. And it was in the wildness of horses that the cave dwellers first began to think of them as domestic. Horses began to be useful to humans when they were portrayed as useless, as decorations on the wall. They became HORSE then, something more than just an animal to chase and catch and kill and eat and skin and strip. And in that moment—which lasted thousands of years—they were placed both within and beyond human control. This is the paradox coming back onto itself like a Möbius strip: horses became wild when they were domesticated into art.

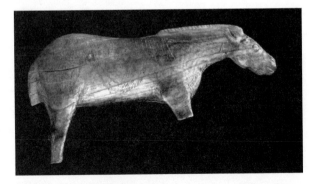

The Horse of Lourdes, carved out of a mammoth's tusk some 15,000 years ago, was found in a cave at Lourdes, France.

"In wildness is the preservation of the world," said Henry David Thoreau. But wildness is a condition that only humans understand. The Nigerian writer Wole Soyinka, exasperated by those who were trying to identify the essence of everything African in the concept of "negritude," said, "The tiger does not go about proclaiming its 'tigritude.' It just pounces." The horse just runs. For all of these original artists, the spirit of a horse was embodied in movement, or in the potential for it.

The movement of horses has fascinated humans from the beginning of time, and anyone who works with horses is always watching the way they move. Watching horses is a lot like reading; you need to learn how to do it. Many of us might admire the delicate curves and shapes of an Arabic script, and the ingenious forms of a Chinese ideogram, but that is not the same as knowing how to read them.

With horses, there are two things we learn to pay attention to. The first is simple: horses don't proclaim their horsiness to tigers and wolves. They just run away. That's the natural part of being a horse, prey to large cats and dogs.

Horses can fight, of course, kicking and biting with damaging and sometimes deadly accuracy. But their best bet has always been flight. That is why, in so many of our myths, the horses fly. "Horse" comes from a word meaning "swift running"—on flat ground, a horse can run at speeds up to forty miles per hour. And horses can run a long way, averaging over ten miles per hour over a hundred miles; among the Kazaks there are records of horses traveling over thirty miles in under two hours. Not every horse can do this, of course, but some can—and all horses secretly measure themselves against those.

The second thing is more subtle. It has to do with quality rather than quantity, with style rather than speed, with grace rather than power. Horses are the gymnasts of the grasslands, and from the beginning, first of all in those cave paintings, they have always been judged for the way they move, not just how fast or how high but how well, how wonderfully well. Or not. As with all judgments, there are sometimes disagreements; but it is surprising how often people agree. Such people are the ones who watch horses, rather than simply see them. And we can all learn how to do that, even if we only learn the basics.

In South Africa, the traditional !Xhosa praise singers

are called *imbongi*. Asked how they interpret motives and manners—the human version of movement—so quickly and confidently, one of them replied, "We watch. *Imbongi* means 'eyes.'"

Imbongi doesn't mean that, in fact. But it should. And so should whatever word we use to describe those who praise horses—our cave painters and contemporary photographers, old plowmen and young horsewomen, plains Indians and cowboys on the pampas, and professional tamers and trainers. We talk about horse whisperers and the ones who listen to horses—and the best of them are amazing—but all good horse trainers, from draft to dressage, from the circus ring to the racetrack, have something in common: they watch. They pay attention. Good horse trainers make the horse do what they want by the quality of their attention.

Yup'ik fishers in Alaska tell how they were taught as youngsters to listen to stories about fishing trips in kayaks offshore so carefully that if a fly landed on their nose they were not to brush it off, because if they lost their concentration and didn't learn the words exactly right, in exactly the right order, they might miss the harbor or offend the spirits or both, when they were older and out on the water. That's what it's like to be around good horsemen and horsewomen. They will listen to you and talk to you, but all along they watch the horse. Like those Yup'ik fishers, they know that at any moment they may find themselves lost in dangerous waters.

Watching is what everyone learns to do around horses. As Yogi Berra said, you can observe a lot by watching. If horses think—and we have much reason to believe they do—then they almost certainly think in pictures, and by association. So it is natural that understanding horses would first and last be a matter of watching them. Marshall McLuhan once said that by way of the meaningless sign linked to the meaningless sound we have built the shape and meaning of the world. Communication with horses, like that between humans, is built around a set of signs and sounds that are like an unknown language to the ignorant and uneducated, but make perfect sense to those who have learned to read and listen. And unlike our other languages, this one is universal across cultures, and it doesn't change with time.

The greatest horse tamers and trainers demonstrate this: the Hittite horsemaster Kikkuli, who wrote in Sanskrit around 1350 BCE; or the Greek Xenophon, born circa 430 BCE in Athens, whose writings were enormously influential throughout the classical world, and still ring true; or Kautilya from India, writing just after Alexander the Great's death in 323 BCE. In modern times there were Federico Caprilli and William Key (handler of Beautiful Jim Key, the "educated horse") and Margaret Cabell Self. Great contemporaries include Tom Dorrance, Ray Hunt, Vicki Hearne, Monty Roberts, and Buck Brannaman. And there is John Jennings, one of Canada's great three-day event riders (cross-country, show jumping, and dressage) in the 1960s and 1970s; and Reg Greer from Mulmur Township in the rural farmland of Ontario, who has been picking up feet since the 1920s. They all watch horses. And horses watch back. "They are the most watchful creatures alive," said John Bell, observing wild horses in Mongolia in 1719.

Listening to horses is important, too, and maybe even whispering sweet nothings. Most people who work well with horses spend a lot of time talking to them, knowing that horses interpret the various sounds of the human voice with remarkable accuracy.

Great trainers become famous not because their horses win this or that race, nor because they gentle this or that giant—though they often do both—but because they cross the line between the human and the non-human. We do that every day when we read a book and make an imaginary world come to life, or when we pray for change in the world around us. It also happens on horseback, or with our hands on the lines. We enter the horse's world, with its own grammar and syntax, its own codes and conventions. This is no more mysterious than a foreign language when we first see or hear it. But it can transform us; and as we learn the new language we find ourselves thinking and feeling differently without even realizing it.

I have been around horses a lot in my life. Mostly, I have stayed on the ground. Sometimes I have been put there by a horse, and occasionally, while I was down there, I've been stomped on, kicked, bitten, boxed in, bullied about, and once I was bounced along the trail for a half mile when I got my foot caught in a rope trying to tail up a couple of pack horses and some yellowjackets came and spooked them.

Anybody who has spent much time around horses, including those who talk about how horses heal us, has stories like this. Horses give us a lot of bruises and broken bones, and nobody who has worked around horses under-estimates their capacity to cripple us.

So their power to heal us sometimes seems only fair. That said, horses can't cure us of all our ills, especially some of those that they bring about. But they do seem to be able to save us from ourselves, not by offering us New Age medicine but by demanding a kind of old-fashioned concentration, similar to that practiced by meditative regimes throughout the world, and with the same familiar stages: composing ourselves in the place we find ourselves in, surrendering our ego, and seeking a moment—no more—of sudden rightness. This takes us into the company of the first person to watch a horse and to wonder at its power and its presence. It's holy ground. It's also dangerous territory.

If we don't acknowledge this we will get nowhere with horses, and we may get hurt. We will also have trouble accepting that something deeply human and spiritual was happening when the Navajo said no, when Bobby Attachie and his people rebuilt their herd of horses after that winter, and when those Paleolithic hunters painted their pictures. That "something" is as essential to humans as running is essential to horses. It has to do with survival, with maintaining the dignity of life when death is just around the corner. It is a way of turning survival into a form of sovereignty, of pushing back reality—a predator, in one form or another—that has the capacity to overwhelm. It is a way of keeping the faith, faith in the power of the imagination to transform reality even if it cannot change it. For the Indians at Fort St. John, restoring the herd was like restoring a work of art, which may be in our custody for a while but whose ultimate ownership is beyond us. That's why selling horses (and even stealing them, some would say) is alright, just as it is with works of art. They don't really belong to anyone, though we often hold on to them with fierce determination, even trying to take them with us when we die—as thousands of years of burial traditions remind us.

Humans have known this about horses from time immemorial, and that knowledge comes back to us, slowly but surely, when we are around horses a lot. Horses have always represented something between here-and-now and then-and-there, and between places and peoples. John Jennings talks about how the moment of suspension is the moment that matters on horseback, the moment between gathering in and moving out, between the rhythms of the horse's movement and your own, between the earth and the air. The great rodeo cowboys say the same thing.

This is the language of meditation. It is the language artists use as well, though they often describe it as the moment when the real and the imagined come together. Whatever language we use, it's there in the movement of a horse and rider, both concentrated and cavalier (symbolized by the mandatory one hand waving free in a rodeo ride), bringing together the clarity of a flying change of leads with the mystery of how it happened, and hovering between surrender and control.

Having control over the horse was something that compelled those cave painters too, for there was undoubtedly magic at work, a calling up of the powers that rule the natural world. Horses were an important source of food to early humans, so anything that would help manage those herds was crucial. As always, the poets and painters were as important as the hunters and gatherers.

The habit of hunting itself goes deep into human consciousness. Whether we like it or not, for tens of thousands of years it has been part of our place in the natural world. We are predators, and, as such, we try to take control. But we also know about surrender. We learn early that there are some things we cannot control, and must surrender to. The weather. Disease. Death. Religion teaches us to accept such things. Science shows us we don't always have to. Working with horses is a blend of both.

Humans began to hunt horses when the world was frozen over. They are not particularly easy to catch, as anyone who has tried to catch one in even a small corral will appreciate. Expand that to a mountain valley, or to the open prairie, and you've got a big challenge. We use helicopters and trucks and all-terrain vehicles to run down herds of wild horses these days, and often we still don't succeed. Our Ice Age ancestors were on foot, and their lives depended on their success in the hunt.

And, like many other animals, horses are often gone before we even know they are there, for they see and hear and smell and feel some things better than we do. But at the end of the day, since they don't hide very well, all they can do is run, very fast and apparently (when you are chasing them) forever. Those early hunters had their work cut out for them.

Horse herds are hierarchical, and the herd's survival depends on individuals obeying the rules.

Horses tend to run in groups of about a half dozen, sometimes more, at least until they are frightened, and that increased the hunters' odds significantly if they could catch the horses by surprise, or corner them. Humans, like many predators, have always been good at cornering prey. Later, when hunting was mostly a thing of the past, we invented a game where that's all we did. It was called war, and it should come as no surprise that we used horses for it.

Horses are into family values, just like humans; and their natural instinct is to keep the family—the herd—together. But humans have another instinct, for another kind of community—the pack. Packs are like business enterprises rather than families, the business being hunting.

And wolves and lions—or our ancestors—on a hunt are like workers going to the job site.

Humans understand both ways of being. They live and feel at home in families, or herds, like horses; and they go to work and play in packs, like wolves. In early days, they used their understanding of herds to hunt all sorts of animals from antelope and elephants to horses. And they used their understanding of packs to organize the hunt. Like any good predator, our ancestors realized that one principle covered many practices and could help them catch many animals.

But they noticed certain things about horses—for example, that herds of horses were small, especially in comparison to elk and buffalo herds, and that in every herd of horses there would be a mare in charge. And if you could get that mare to lead the others into a box canyon, or—with luck and good management—into some kind of makeshift corral, with grass, they would settle down to eat. And then you could kill them more easily, or at least corner them without having to run all over the place trying to catch them. Our ancestors would have observed too that small groups of younger stallions also stayed together, in a bachelor group away from a herd of mares who would be followed by a single older stallion. The mares decided where to go, and when; their stallion ran along behind. The human hunters would have found out, probably painfully, that this older stallion didn't take kindly to having anyone interfere with his harem. Maybe they taunted him, and tempted him into a fight to distract him. But he knew that game, and as often as not they were probably badly bitten or kicked more than a few times. Even small horses—and most of them were small in those early days—could be deadly.

Horses, like humans, have habits, and some of these didn't make it any easier for the hunters. They eat most of the time, and they sleep very little. Unless they are young or in foal, horses need only about four hours of sleep every day, which they often take in snatches as short as ten or fifteen minutes. That comes of being the hunted rather than the hunter. Cats, on the other hand, sleep up to sixteen hours a day. For four million years, horses couldn't sleep for long stretches because they would be easy prey. They needed to keep watch constantly, like sailors at sea. Even if they were dozing, they might need to be off and running in a couple of seconds. So mostly they slept standing up, and in the daytime. One of the advantages of having four legs is that you *can* sleep that way, and you can get in motion quickly by simply shifting your weight to your hind legs, where the horsepower is. Occasionally, hidden in the middle of a herd and surrounded by their mothers, the young ones will lie on their side. But as they get older they do this less often.

And horses cultivate surprise. Humans and horses, like all predators and their prey, share the surprise. But they are on different sides of it. That is why horses are always more or less on the move, however slowly. Along with other herd animals, they are the original nomads.

～

As the climate changed and the glaciers retreated, some 10,000 years ago, people were gradually able to live more predictably, following the seasons and the availability of feed for the animals. Herding some animals rather than hunting them became a better way of tapping into the natural rhythm.

From a horse's point of view this wasn't all good news, since now the humans would come and cull—which is to say, kill—the older animals, and some of the young ones. But that happened anyway, sooner or later, in the wild; so tame was not so terrible. And horses held in herds for human purposes—originally meat and milk—were better protected from other predators.

From the humans' perspective, horses were relatively low-maintenance animals, and especially good in cold weather where their hooves are well adapted to scraping away snow. Sheep and cattle, on the other hand, use their noses, which in hard weather become bloody and sore, especially if the snow cover is deep. And in any weather, horses are food specialists, picking and choosing the parts of the plant they want with elegant dexterity. When food of high nutritional value is available—like the alfalfa on the plains of ancient Media in Persia where Herodotus's "sacred horses" were bred, or the fields of clover that produced the "heavenly horses of Ferghana" in China—horses grow larger and stronger. When they return to leaner rations they revert to smaller sizes, as the Spanish horses did when they came to the Americas.

But people soon realized that as a source of meat and milk, cattle and sheep and pigs could be bred for large rumps, "cobby" (round) backs, and big udders more easily than horses. Breeding was one of the great discoveries of humankind; by breeding, humans could reproduce and reinforce the qualities they wanted in an animal. They could improve nature, making it over according to their own wants and needs. In its own way, this is what nature has always done, as Darwin realized when he developed his theory of evolution after the model of the domestic breeders of his time. Selection, natural or not, is what it's all about.

Perhaps because it is one of the ways we can exercise some control over the natural world, breeding has become one of our great obsessions. It has also nourished our debilitating preoccupation with race. This didn't begin with our fascination with horse breeds, but it was certainly encouraged by it.

Among other things, horse breeding created an arbitrary set of categories that exaggerated distinctions while ignoring commonalities. In many ways, different breeds are more like different dialects—or sometimes just different accents—than different languages. Breeding also created a whole new set of confusions about the relationship between nurture and nature, confusions that we then brought to matters of race. The determination of many cultures to maintain the purity of their horse breeds— often, astonishingly, on pain of death to the outlaw breeder—underscores our unease about miscegenation, and our sometimes pathological convictions about the value of certain lines of heritage over others.

Fashion counts for a lot here, as it does in all questions of race and color. Color is an especially interesting category in this regard, because its significance with regard to horses is so widely misunderstood (just as it is with humans). In horses, color does have some bearing on an animal's resistance to sunburn and saddle sores; but it is mostly the case, as an old adage has it, that "fat—some would say 'fit'—is the best color" for a horse.

That said, different colors have their enthusiasts, and fads are constantly changing. As one writer put it, reflecting on the change that took place in the popularity of particular draft horses in the United States in the 1930s, when over two-thirds were Percherons: "There was a rapidly growing sorrel and roan cloud on the Percheron horizon, destined to challenge and eventually wrest the number one spot from the blacks and greys. The sorrel with white mane and tail became the Cadillac of colors with farmers." Arguments over the best color for a horse began with the cave painters, and continued in every horse culture the world has ever known.

In the eighteenth century in England, horses even set the pace for the purity of the peerage, establishing a lineage of nobility that is still the hallmark of horse racing, and fiercely maintained. The *General Stud Book* that first listed Thoroughbred lines, compiled by one James Weatherby in 1791, preceded *Burke's Peerage*, the account book of the English nobility (who owned most of these horses) by thirty-five years. Both effectively determined appropriate matches.

This preoccupation with making matches, a central feature of eighteenth- and nineteenth-century European society, is reflected in its most popular literary form, the novel. It applied just as much to horses as it did to humans, and it is alive and well in both communities. Good matches are the topic of conversations in the horse barn as much as they are at the country club—and they are all about breeds and breeding.

☙

Early in the history of human civilization, on the prairie grasslands and boreal forests of central Asia, horses became like the buffalo to the Blackfoot—both suppliers of goods and sacred gods. All gods tend to be like that—

the source of everything that is needed for a full life, materially as well as spiritually. For the aboriginal hunters and gatherers of the world, subsistence was never about merely getting by; it was spiritual surplus, an original form of affluence. Clothing and shelter, many implements and tools, and some playthings, were made from the flesh and bones, as well as the feet and skin, of horses, and it was hardly surprising that their spirits began to grace these gifts of life.

Then there came a time, probably very early in their relationship, when horses began to be part of the *death* of humans, and of the ceremonies commemorating it and controlling its mystery. The traditions of sacrifice that characterize so many societies to this day, including Judeo-Christian ones, remind us of how much death remains a part of life.

We aren't exactly sure how or when this first happened; but it did happen almost everywhere, from China to India, from Russia to the Middle East, from Europe to Africa, and all across the Americas. We do know that the role of horses in burial ceremonies goes as far back as the Bronze Age, when humans recognized that the horse had given itself to the people, and that this gift—which was

Funerary terra-cotta figurine (China, Han dynasty)

spiritual as well as material—must be respected. To do so properly, people had to observe certain conventions, first of all in capturing and killing, and then in caring for the horse. A bond was created between humans and horses that has never ceased, and that found a later form in the ceremonial traditions of chivalry.

This special bond began in the simplest of ways. Horse meat was a staple of the diet in cultures throughout Asia and Europe for tens of thousands of years, and certain types of horse meat were prized by the privileged. Why it became unpalatable to so many peoples—while others eat it to this day—is fascinating. The major reason was competing religious practices. From the Copper Age peoples of the Caucasus to the Celts of Ireland, sacrifices and ceremonies involving horses—including drinking and even bathing in horses' blood—were common. And this was a problem for those who were trying to maintain their own sacrificial practices. In 732, Pope Gregory III outlawed the eating of horsemeat, and for reasons that aren't all that different, Buddhism prohibited it, Islam discouraged it, and Hindus simply refrained.

A second reason was more practical: once humans began to use horses as beasts of burden, replacing oxen and onagers (Asiatic asses) for carrying and pulling and then for driving and riding, they became too valuable to eat for meat.

Now horses became partners in the hunt, no longer the hunted. Humans had first hunted with dogs; but well-trained horses were both more effective and more fun—and occasionally more dangerous. Whether mounted or driven (and often accompanied by dogs), they made the hunt into a relatively efficient way of obtaining meat, as well as a sport that appealed to many different cultures, from the Assyrians and Egyptians—who both hunted a wide range of animals—to the Macedonian fox-hunters and the medieval European stag-hunters.

Much more recently, horses have become a symbol of animal rights, with thoughts and feelings comparable to those of human beings. We can see a spectacular example of this with the phenomenon known as Beautiful Jim Key, the "educated horse" (as he was advertised), trained and taken on tour by the former slave and Civil War veteran Dr. William Key at the beginning of the twentieth century. Jim Key became a center of attraction around the United States, astounding audiences with his ability to calculate and compute and even to spell out A-L-I-C-E R-O-O-S-E-V-E-L-T L-O-N-G-W-O-R-T-H to President Theodore Roosevelt's daughter (a year *before* she married Nicholas Longworth) when she visited St. Louis on the opening day of the Louisiana Purchase Exposition in 1904. By being so surprisingly like a human—and a rather intelligent one at that—Jim Key helped the animals' rights advocates argue against the slaughter of anything with four legs, and generated an enthusiasm for cuddling rather than killing. His remarkable career was tempered by the tale of a German horse called Clever Hans, who solved difficult mathematical problems—including square roots—written on a blackboard, until it was discovered that he was responding to the subtlest body language and breathing changes in the person posing the questions—thereby proving he was an ordinary horse with a horse's extraordinary abilities.

Almost every culture retains some elements of what we might call horse worship, with horseshoes and horse brasses reminding us of their place in folklore. But funeral ceremonies still provide some of the most haunting images of how humans venerated—and feared—horses. One of the most compelling is the head-and-hoof horse burial figure, found from the Paleolithic age to the present. In early times, it consisted of the skin of a horse hung over an extended pole, a sort of sacred scarecrow. The bones of the head, the tail, and the feet were left in the carcass to

Bronze figurine from an incineration burial (found in the Czech Republic, dated between the 10th and 6th century BCE).

maintain the shape of the horse, ensuring that it hung properly and, in the tradition of burial representations all over the world, simultaneously evoked both life and death—or, in the case of these horses, that moment of suspension between earth and air that is their ultimate gift of grace.

Herodotus describes such a burial among the Scythians, and there are many others that have been excavated over the last century. And this wasn't a practice that died with the people who first used bronze and copper 6,000 years ago. The Blackfoot burial traditions in Crop Eared Wolf's time continued this tradition with the sacrifice of horses routinely accompanying the death of leaders. Before a horse was killed—in those latter days by shooting or sometimes strangling it—he might be painted with pictographs representing his owner's exploits; his tail would then be braided and tied in a ball, and his mane adorned with feathers. After the horse's death, it was ashes to ashes and dust to dust, for only the spirit of the horse accompanied the deceased, though usually the braided mane and tail, and occasionally the whole horse, would be put on the platform or into the ground. The Nez Perce were known to have skinned and stuffed horses and set them up as grave monuments, and other tribes hung the skins at the grave. In Kazakstan to this day, a deceased owner's horse is slaughtered at a special ceremony a year after his death, and horse races are held so that the deceased can listen to the thunder of hooves.

On the central Russian steppes near where the Dneiper and the Don Rivers flow into the Black Sea, at a place called Dereivka in what is now Ukraine, a stallion that was buried some 6,000 years ago has become as much a cult figure to modern archeologists as it may have been to the people who buried it. From evidence here and at other sites in the area, there is reason to think that this may be where horses were first domesticated, since it appears from teeth wear that this "cult stallion" wore a bit in its mouth. If we accept this—and there is convincing evidence—then we need to consider the possibiliy that this was also the time and place where Indo-European, the mother tongue from which languages as different as English and Russian and Persian and Hindi evolved, was last spoken by a single speech community. So what we may have is another suspended moment, in which the first horseback rider was also the last to live in a world in which people could all understand each other.

☙

Still, many people question when and where humans first brought horses into the intimate circle of their lives, domesticating them in the family. Some say it was in northeast China, near the Tian Shan Mountains; others suggest the Ural Mountains in what is now Kazakstan. And still others settle for Ukraine. There is also no clear proof which breeds were first domesticated, since it appears as though the two or three main lines of ancestral horses—the Mongolian wild horse, the proto-Arab, and the Tarpan pony—had long since ceased to be the founding mothers and fathers of separate families, and mixed breeds had started to emerge. But there is evidence—though like almost everything to do with horses, it is disputed—that humans began to domesticate horses as far back as Neolithic times, nearly 10,000 years ago. What *is* certain is that the special relationship between horses and humans began early.

Slowly, but surely, a sense of common cause would have developed, beginning with the move from hunting to herding. In herds, there are relationships of both family and friends, especially among the mares and foals. Humans would have noticed, and above all the children, who often teach the old folks anyway.

Maybe our desire to make friends with horses began this way, with a young girl and a foal:

> The girl was quick and graceful, dressed in a horsehair jacket and leggings of reindeer hide that her mother had dried and tanned, and lace-up boots made of skin from the hind legs of a horse, with rawhide laces.

> The mare was creamy gray, "the color of a cloudless sky" in Kazak. She had a new foal, which had come into the world over by the woods the previous night. Horses almost always foal at night, because that's when predators are least likely to notice. And foals learn fast—in just twenty-four hours, they can do almost everything an adult can: walk, talk, and even see at night, which is important for horses since they are nocturnal by nature.

> When the girl stepped out of her yurt—a felt tent, with a wooden door painted blue—and came over to the mare and her day-old foal in the grassy field on the other side of the creek, the foal looked right at her. The girl was happy, because she had learned that one

can tell a lot by looking into a horse's eyes; if they are always looking into the distance, they will never be your friend. The mare (who was paying no attention to the girl) licked her foal all over, and nibbled at his neck, making her teeth into a kind of curry comb, and then the foal nuzzled up to get some milk.

The girl knew all about that milk. Her mother was known for the *koumiss* she brewed, the fermented drink made from the curd of mare's milk that was a special part of the people's diet out there on the steppes. Her grandmother said it would cure almost everything. It could also make you feel silly. Her mother always made it in a skin bag, pouring the milk in first, then putting in a fresh piece of horse skin, or the dried remnants of the last brew, and whipping it all up for what seemed to the girl like hours.

In the spring, when the first mare was milked, they would have a celebration and all the women would drink some of the koumiss after thanking *Kambar-ata*, the protector of horses. Later, the women would have a wrestling match. It was gross, but fun to watch, and they all cheered on their mothers. The girl's mother had told her that she would teach her how to make koumiss so that she could get a good husband. There were thirty words for koumiss, and only one for husband.

The girl had heard the story about the person who first milked a mare, back in the old, old days when humans first learned how to sneak up on a horse. It sure wasn't easy, because horses can tell when someone is walking nearby. They feel it through their feet. Hooves are where the horse's spirit dwells, her mother would say. A hoof is like a second heart in a horse, absorbing compression every time she stands or moves by squeezing blood back up through her veins.

Every day for weeks, the girl walked beside the foal, and petted him, and combed his mane, and scratched his favorite spot (right up where his front leg joined his ribs), and the foal would stretch out his neck with his head to one side—as though he was laying his head on someone's shoulder—and get a faraway look in his eyes. After talking, the key to making friends with a horse is scratching. It's the basis of all good horse training, and it's how horses make friends with each other in the field.

So the foal itched, and the girl scratched, and before long they were friends. And when the foal was several months old, she fed him handfuls of grass that she had picked, shoving them into his mouth because the foal didn't seem to want them. First, he just spat them out; then after a while he ate some. Finally the girl stole some grains of wheat from a wooden bowl that her mother kept hidden away, which turned out to be a really good idea, because after that all she needed to do was make a rattling sound and the foal would run over to her.

Day after day, week after week, month after month into the early fall, the girl followed the foal around, patting him on the back, scratching his neck, combing his mane, while the foal, for his part, began to see the girl as *his* responsibility, and would go looking for her when she wasn't there.

Then one day the girl decided to throw a pretty blanket over the foal, one of the old ones that her mother had woven years before. The foal shook himself, and threw it off. So the girl picked the blanket up, put it over her own shoulders to show the foal how it was done and how pretty it looked, then patted the foal's neck and tried again. The foal scampered away, but this time the blanket didn't come off.

Over and over again, for three weeks, the girl did this. And then one time, just before they moved for the winter camp, she put the blanket over the foal, scratched him where he liked it, did a little skip like she'd seen the ducks do before they hopped onto a rock, and jumped on his back, holding to his mane like there was no tomorrow. The foal stopped eating, turned his head, looked at her as though to say "it took you long enough". . . and then went back to the business of clipping the fall grass, which was wet and dry all at the same time.

Chapter 3

ON THE MOVE
AROUND THE GLOBE

How Horse Travel and Transport
Changed the World

In 1872, the former governor of California, Leland Stanford, made a bet with some friends about whether a horse has all four feet off the ground at any moment when it is at a trot. It was an ancient argument—the Egyptians had wondered the same thing thousands of years earlier—but Stanford had an advantage. The technology for watching moving subjects was finally catching up with the horse.

Phases of the Trot (Eadweard Muybridge, 1887)

It was the age of photography, and Stanford commissioned a photographer named Eadweard Muybridge to settle the bet. At that time, every photographic plate—which was made of glass—had to be wet-coated just before a picture was taken, so it was impossible to take shots in rapid succession. Impossible, that is, with *one* camera. So Muybridge used twenty-four single lens cameras, alongside twelve large ones (each with twelve lenses), timing the exposures with mechanical and electromagnetic clockwork accurate to 1/6000 of a second. At the time, half a second was considered instantaneous.

In 1882, the results were published, and Stanford won

his bet. A trotting horse has all its feet off the ground twice during each stride.

⫷

When Muybridge settled the bet, he set in motion a serious scientific study of the way animals move. As so often with horses, it was those who were skilled at watching them, including Muybridge and other photographers, who did most to explain the mysteries of their movement, and within a decade, photographic bulletins were routinely advising how to photograph the gaits of a horse.

In 1899, Muybridge published what has become a classic, *Animals in Motion*; but his popular influence had to do with the history of technology rather than the history of science. He invented a way of printing his photographs on a glass disc and spinning the disk to project them on a screen, which he called a "zoopraxiscope"; it was the original motion-picture projector. Thomas Edison took some of the ideas for his "kinetiscope" from Muybridge, and he also took advantage of the recent invention of celluloid photographic film to replace the glass plates. The two of them even talked about adding a phonograph to the moving picture system to provide sound. . . .

So movies began with horses. This was appropriate, since movement is what horses are all about. Movement, music, and dance. In music, movement is described in terms of rhythm; with horses, people talk about gaits. We watch horses the way we listen to music: first the rhythm, as we tap our toes and listen to our hearts; then the melody, the direction and flow.

The basic gaits, or rhythms, of horses are familiar ones: the walk, the trot, and the gallop. Some people insist on the difference between these "natural" gaits and those that are "nurtured"—such as the pace, in which the same-side (or lateral) legs move forward at the same time, and the rack, a flashy four-beat gait in which each of the feet strikes the ground at a slightly different time. But some say that they *are* natural to horses, just latent in most and made manifest with encouragement or instruction. Our modern word for training—education—means "leading forth" and "developing," one implication being that the potential is already there.

The Icelandic horse, which was brought to Iceland in the ninth century by the Vikings and bred true for a thousand years, illustrates the difficulty of making such distinctions. In addition to the walk, trot, and gallop, it has two unusual gaits that come naturally to it: the tölt, a four-beat lateral gait that is very useful for traveling over uneven, rough ground, and the flying pace, which is unique to the Icelandic horse.

What does make a horse a horse and not a pony? Is it feeding, or breeding? To some, the simple answer is that a pony is any horse under 14 $\frac{1}{2}$ hands (a "hand" being four inches); but then things get more complicated. Measured that way, the "cow pony" that cowboys ride is usually a horse, while the Icelandic horse, by that standard, is really a pony; and yet, defined by its weight-carrying abilities, bone structure, and overall weight, it is nothing short of a horse. In turn, the "wild horses" of the world are often pony size; and so ponies are frequently described as typically less refined, hardier, more independent than horses. But just try to tell that to some of the horses on the rodeo circuit. Size matters, and it doesn't matter at all.

The canter—from "Canterbury gallop," the easy pace at which medieval pilgrims were said to ride to the cathedral town—is sometimes called a fourth "natural" gait, though others call it a "collected" gallop, one in which the front legs and the back legs are more under the horse (like a closed accordion) than extended out. But almost every distinction between schooled movements and those that are innate breaks down as soon as you see an actual horse doing this or that. Over the centuries so many horses have been bred to particular gaits that training and genetics are now hard to distinguish; one of the many reasons horses are so fascinating to humans is that they provide such a range of examples of the interdependence of nature and nurture. And pretty much everything about them can generate an argument, like the continuing controversy over how useful it is for a rider to collect a horse before turning or jumping. It depends on the premium you put on the horse doing what comes naturally to it— and on your perception of exactly what that is. The best riders reach a compromise that is specific to each horse and each situation, the challenge being to control and release the energy of the horse at just the right moment —so that both horse and rider achieve a state of balance in a covenant of wonder.

The difference in gaits comes down to rhythm, first of all. But it also has to do with the ways in which the legs move in relation to each other, either diagonally or laterally. This, patterned against the beat of each different gait, provides a form of melody. The walk has four beats, with the legs moving in more or less diagonal sequence, while the gallop has three beats, picked up in the theme music that often accompanied Diablo or Trigger or Silver or Champion galloping across the western plains in the movies back in the middle of the last century. In between, there are the trot and the pace, both of which have two beats: in the trot, the diagonal legs move together; in the pace, it's the lateral legs.

And then there are the four-beat lateral gaits, such as the running walk and the slow pace (which some American Saddlebreds display, though the most stylized running walk is done by the Tennessee Walking Horse), as well as the *paso* gaits of the Paso Fino and the Peruvian Paso, which are close to a fast canter. There is a spectacular version called the *sobreandando*, which has a paddling action—sometimes called dishing—in the forelegs; but (of course!) there are disagreements about this. Some don't like paddling, dismissing it as an unwelcome trait, and in some horses it certainly is a fault. But then again, Muhammad, who cherished horses, called one of his favorites Swimmer because he liked the way he lifted his feet in that same paddling motion when he galloped. In any case, these pace and paso gaits are generally easy on the rider, and most were developed to provide comfortable rides over long distances. Some say that the easygoing western lope is also a separate gait, hovering near a four-beat rhythm between a running walk and a smooth canter.

We know little about the gaits that were common 3,000 or 4,000 years ago, when long distances were the norm. Almost all our evidence is from paintings and inscriptions and carvings and other forms of visual representation, and these are usually highly stylized. They are also posed, rather than moving, pictures. But we can assume—because horses haven't changed much over the last few thousand years (a mere blink in the four or five million years since equus first made its appearance on earth)—that the early gaits were probably very similar to those we know today. Modern equestrian sports, from the three-day event to the racetrack and from endurance competitions to the rodeo circuit, also give us a good idea of what would have worked under different circumstances.

Some things we can infer: a knight in shining armor, for instance, would almost certainly have moved no faster than an amble, since the horse would have been carrying up to six hundred pounds of rider and rigging. On the other hand, from our knowledge of the distances they covered, the terrain they traveled, and the time they took, the great horse warriors such as Alexander the Great and Genghis Khan must have ridden at something between a running walk and a slow canter. Accounts of them by their enemies emphasize ferocious speed; but this would have been when they were sweeping through the enemy camps, leaving everyone on the ground in a state of shock.

As Stanford's bet confirms, this is the stuff of endless arguments among horse people, for it is notoriously difficult to make precise distinctions where movement is concerned. After all, the arguments about horses began way back when people knew them very well, riding or driving them all the time. But perhaps most of the ancient folk were like many of us today with cars: we use them pretty much every day, and we try to look after them fairly well—but we have next to no idea how they actually work.

⤳

Working well is one thing. Looking good is another, and it has always been important to horses. Like humans, they need to look good in order to feel good. Some people will say that horses don't care how they look. But these are people who don't care about horses.

Horses are our original style setters, acutely sensitive to how they look and how they're being looked at. They have good hair days and bad hair days, just like us, and bad hair days can be really bad. So grooming is important. If you are a horse out there in a herd, you have to rely on another horse—one of the family or a friend—to groom you. In fact, friends often trump family when it comes to mutual grooming in a herd of horses.

When humans began looking after horses, they quickly took over the grooming. Then they dressed the horses up. There were those burial arrangements first; and then apparel for the living horses got more and more elaborate. In all cultures, including ancient ones, there is evidence of making up horses to make them look good. Even the horse paintings of 15,000 and 30,000 years ago have their stylizations, with tapered muzzles and white nostrils and shoulder stripes and other fashionable touches.

The Calgary Stampede, one of the great rodeos of the West, had its start in 1912. It became one of *the* festivals of the western plains, and Crop Eared Wolf—who had become head chief of the Blackfoot by this time—came with two thousand of his people, and they rode in full regalia in the parade through town before setting up their teepees around the Stampede grounds. Their horses were decorated with their best blankets and saddles and bridles and breech bands, all beaded and inlaid, and one horse even had a horse mask on, and two had feathers attached to their brow bands, which protected them in battle. This is an ancient tradition. Near a place called Pazyryk in Siberia there are tombs from the third century BCE in which horses were buried with felt masks and head dresses on, almost certainly a legacy of the great Scythian horse culture of centuries earlier, and some of them had ornamental bits that would impress today's most extroverted punk rockers or piercers.

Fashions are, by definition, bound to time and place; but one thing seems to be common across the ages—setting the model in motion down the runway (with haute couture) or on the road (with a carriage). From jousting tournaments to fox hunts, from the parade ground to the conformation show, humans draped their horses with clothes and jewelry and then got them moving.

We have taken horses into the heart of many of our sacred as well as our secular ceremonies, often choosing one of a certain color—white or black or gray, for example—for special occasions such as weddings, coronations, and funerals. And into our myths: the Norse god Odin storms across the skies on Sleipnir, his eight-legged white horse, while in the Bhagavad Gita Krishna, one of the incarnations of Vishnu, drives a cart pulled by two white horses. Amulets called horse brasses have been worn for at least a couple of thousand years to repel the evil eye, especially on triumphal occasions when a malevolent spirit would be most likely to interfere with the good fortune being celebrated. And a horseshoe is nailed over many an entrance to this day.

Krishna and Arjuna Leaving for the Battle
(India, 18th century CE)

It is horses that make the difference in these comings-together. They are the custodians of ceremony for humans, the ones who bring the past into the present and show what the future might hold. Horses have been on parade since the beginnings of time, prancing across the walls of ancient caves, dancing in the circus rings and dressage arenas, drawing the carriages of royalty through the great cities of the world, and running wild in the few spaces we have left open.

≈

It is an open question whether humans rode on horses' backs before they rode in carts behind them. The cart was as important as the rider in our history, and one thing is certain: for a long time, riding *on* horses was what barbarians did; riding *behind* them was the civilized way. In a letter sent by a protocol chief to King Zimri-Lin of the city state of Mari on the Euphrates river around 1780 BCE, the king was advised to ride in a chariot, or perhaps on a donkey—but definitely not on horseback.

The advisor doesn't explain why, though it was probably for a number of reasons, from local fashion to the fact that horses sweat. Also, in a time when horseback riding was not widely practiced in that society and the king might not have much experience, he might fall off or be thrown. Not good for a demigod.

This letter is our earliest written record of horse management, and was composed just before the Asiatic Hyksos overwhelmed Egypt and introduced horses there. The Egyptians, like many peoples at the time, were using donkeys rather than horses for transport and riding, with riders seated well back on the loins of the animal—in the so-called donkey seat—rather than forward behind the withers. We can see the prestige still accorded to donkeys in the region fifteen hundred years later when Jesus rode into Jerusalem on a donkey. But within a few centuries, the prophet Muhammad rode to heaven on a horse.

For a long time, the only people who rode horses were the nomadic tribes, following the seasons and managing their herds of horses for meat and milk, and occasionally raiding their neighbors. Homer, writing about 3,000 years ago, referred to them as mare-milkers living in perpetual darkness, and that darkness was cultural as well as geographical. The "raw" rode horses, roaming here and there in the wild; and the "cooked" were pulled along behind them, driving from town to town.

Of course, carts were used by the wanderers, too—after all, they knew pretty much everything that horses could do, and they would certainly have recognized the advantages of putting the horse before the cart; the great nomadic peoples of the Far East, who probably had horses domesticated as early as 3000 BCE, bred large horses for precisely that purpose.

A horse can pull more than she can carry; but she can go more places carrying than pulling. So packing supplies on a horse's back would have happened early in human history. That raises another question: whether the first thing on a horse's back was a pack or a person—maybe a young child or an old person, strapped onto a reliable old mare? We'll never know. Certainly, the appearance of a person—the rider—moving above and behind would initially be very frightening for a horse, because that's precisely where a big cat would come from. And further, horses like what packers call quiet loads, loads that don't shift about, loads that are always well balanced. Even the best riders can't claim to be able to do that all the time, and the great American jockey Eddie Arcaro, asked about the choice between live weight and dead weight (put on a horse to even the handicap), voted for dead weight, properly placed. So it's likely the first horse carried a pack rather than a person.

Even after everyone else had mounted up, the identification of so-called barbaric hordes of hunters and herders with horseback riding and so-called civilized agricultural societies with farm carts and fancy carriages continued. It was fostered by figures like Attila the Hun—a descendant of the ancient Mongolians of the Gobi desert—who invaded the Western world in the fifth century CE. Of course, he may also have introduced the stirrup to the West, one of the most civilized of inventions; but that isn't usually part of the story of these barbarians. Theirs were the evil empires of the ancient mind. Yet it was those same barbarians, living on the great grasslands beyond the Black Sea and riding their horses, that eventually transformed settled societies throughout Asia and Europe and Africa.

Although horsemen armed with spears and arrows had been around for centuries, and the Hittites and the Egyptians probably used riders for scouting and carrying messages, what we think of as cavalry regiments came later to the civilized world of the Fertile Crescent, where horses were originally used mostly either for domestic transport or for drawing chariots. It took another thousand years after that letter to King Zimri-Lin for warriors on horse-back, organized into units and deployed in a strategic manner, to come into widespread use in the Middle East.

The change happened first because the battleground changed. Assyria, which controlled a rich farming domain, had been engaged in sporadic annexation of territory for some time; but to the north were mountain ranges inhabited by barbaric hill tribes who weren't about to share their minerals and metals and wood with these civilized intruders. Finding chariots inadequate for that terrain, and made painfully aware by Armenian raiders, among others, of what damage mounted horsemen could do, the

Assyrian war chariot (Nineveh, Assyria, 7th century BCE)

Assyrians formed cavalry units around 900 BCE. Like the Blackfoot after their defeat by the Shoshone, and the Egyptians after being overrun by the Hyksos, the Assyrians said, "we've got to *ride* those horses." And so they began to breed horses suitable for mounted warfare (they had already bred donkeys for a thousand years for peacetime service). In order to supply the necessary stock, Assyria seems also to have introduced the profession of horse traders; *tamken sise*, they called them.

There is a deep contradiction in all this, in which horses were inevitably implicated. Nomads were uncivilized not just because they rode horses but because they did not settle down. That was the accepted line, which has rung down through the millennia. "The history of nearly every race that has advanced from barbarism to civilization has been through the stages of the hunter, the herdsman, the agriculturalist, and finally reaching those of commerce, mechanics and the higher arts," said United States cavalry officer Nelson Miles in 1879, who accepted surrender from the leader of another tribe of "barbaric" horsemen—Chief Joseph and the Nez Perce—in 1877. Then he took all their horses.

Years later, Chief Joseph wrote a letter in which he was philosophic about the treachery that he had come to recognize as part of such dealings, but very particular in his concern about his people's horses. "I believe General Miles would have kept his word if he could have done so," he said. "I do not blame him for what we have suffered since the surrender. I do not know who is to blame." But then he added, "We gave up all our horses—over eleven hundred —and all our saddles—over one hundred—and we have not heard from them since. Someone has got our horses."

When another general, Philip Sheridan, took those of the Cheyenne and the Sioux he called them "worthless horses," foreshadowing the language of the Meriam Report. And yet he made his living on horseback.

This kind of contradiction is standard in the history of horses and humans. In a court case in British Columbia that took place as recently as the 1980s, involving Indians who lived on the other side of the mountains from Bobby Attachie and who were seeking recognition of their land rights, the judge said that, since their ancestors had no horses and no wheeled vehicles, they must have been uncivilized, "roaming from place to place like beasts of the field."

And yet it was precisely those same horses that had *enabled* people to roam from place to place like beasts of the field, to travel to foreign lands like flocks of migrating birds, and to build new cities and cultures. Horses, apparently, are agents of both "barbarism" and "civilization." It all seems to be about our attitude towards wandering versus settling down.

Horses gave people a way to do both: to travel with the seasons and the livestock, hunting and herding; and to settle in more appealing parts of the country, and farm. In one of the best-known of all cowboy songs, "Home on the Range," the opening rhyme catches the contradiction: "O give me a home, where the buffalo roam." While "home" and "roam" are bound together by similar sounds, their senses pull in completely opposite directions. Settling down—and wandering. It's hard to imagine a more basic human opposition, or a more fundamental human condition. Our imaginations take this in every time we sing these lines (composed about 125 years ago), and we remember them not because they tell one truth, but because they tell two contradictory ones. Both wanderers and settlers have shaped our global history.

Migrations of significant groups of people began as the climate continued to warm up and the forests spread northward. Humans, like horses, are savannah animals, and they both must have realized that they shared a love of the foothills and open lands where it was easier to see things, and easier to run away from them. So about 4,000 years ago, a great migratory movement began that transformed the world in a way that was perhaps unparalleled until the modern age. The Aryan peoples—so-called because they all spoke the same family of Indo-European languages, and not because they were from the same "race"—packed up and spread from the steppes of southern Russia to India, to the valleys of the Tigris and the Euphrates, and on to Europe.

For a long time much of Europe has had an antipathy towards "travelers," specifically the gypsy or Roma people whose speech is closely related to that of northwest India and whose nomadic way of life has resulted in their routine persecution since they arrived in Europe around the fifteenth century, reaching a horrific extreme in the Nazi death camps.

But the long association of the gypsies with horses (and caravans, now usually motorized) has also given their way of life a continuing fascination, even to those who are constantly trying to get them to give up their wandering ways and settle down.

☙

Did civilization begin with settling down and farming, or with mounting up and riding? Neither—and both.

Neither, because tens of thousands of years ago hunter-gatherer societies in tundra and desert lands and in the forests and on the seashores developed a wide range of stable and sophisticated traditions—spiritual as well as material—that defined a homeland, one in which they moved from place to place harvesting flora and fauna, without agricultural settlements or horses.

And both, because a fundamental condition of agricultural development since Neolithic times has been to settle down and farm the land with oxen and asses and eventually horses, and then to move on, to plow up other places and unsettle other peoples, often riding there on horses or being pulled by them. This is the story of civilization, as agriculture spread across Asia to Europe and Africa and to the Americas and Australia. It was usually not a cheerful story, since it involved the dispossession and dislocation of hunting and herding peoples. And it was often made possible by horses. Horses have had more influence on the rise and fall of civilizations than any other factor, including the weather.

Was the stage at which humans first began to ride and drive horses the start of "civilization" then, signaling the settling down of people? Or did horseback riding merely reinforce the "barbaric" habits of nomadic life, and nourish an appetite for travel and change and the unsettling influences of global news? Once again, neither and both.

It may be precisely that urge to wander, the urge to roam that makes us human. It is certainly what keeps us alive when conditions become intolerable. It also makes us dangerous when we try to change the conditions to suit ourselves—dangerous to the environment, and to other people. Horses allowed us to become human, to move across the land and to hack and hew the landscape. But they also gave us the ability to destroy lands, and the livelihoods that depended upon them. Horses brought people together, in cultures that shared land and language and livelihood. And moved them apart, so that they began to live differently and speak differently and behave differently.

The other urge—to settle down and make a home for ourselves—seems just as basic. It has created not only agricultural systems that involve subtle and sophisticated collaboration with nature and produce food supplies that sustain large gatherings of people, but also the cities and villages and cathedrals and cottages and temples and factories that, for all their problems, are among humankind's great achievements.

Horses gave humans a way of settling down to farm, and then of defining and defending these farms; and they gave them a way of moving on and opening up new territory. With horses, almost anything seemed possible. Horses transformed the world, literally and figuratively, and although ox and ass first broke the ground, it was the horse that made agriculture much easier and more efficient. And perhaps most significantly, horses made it possible for settlers to get up and go when the spirit—or the threat of starvation—moved them.

Which is the natural state of humans: wandering, or settling down? It's like asking whether climate or culture is the primary condition of constancy and change. Or whether it is nurture or nature that shapes our lives. Horses helped humans negotiate between climate and culture, nurture and nature. And horses helped humans break up the old opposition between wanderers and settlers, in which so many people had invested so much economic and political capital. One of the reasons people hold on to hunting on horseback so stubbornly may be because it reminds them of this.

In the beginning, it was the wanderers who peopled the world. The greatest of them were the nomadic tribes who moved from the steppes of central Asia in a sweep down south to Africa, the Middle East, and India, east into China and west to Europe, and earlier (though this, too, is lost in the mists of time) across the Bering Land Bridge to the Americas.

Inevitably, when some of the people stopped wandering for a while and schooled themselves in the civilities of farming and fixed settlements, they viewed the next wave of horsemen who came sweeping down on them as primitive barbarians. After they had counted their losses, they usually went out to get some horses and learned anew how to use them.

Both wandering and settling down were nourished by curiosity. Probably boredom too, as people got tired of one or the other. But it was curiosity that turned people's minds towards the horizon, and created the remarkable tools that made both staying put and moving on possible.

The use of fibers—plaited grasses and bark, stripped hides, woven hair—was a particularly significant innovation; fibers, almost as much as fire, made it possible to harness natural forces for human purposes. Tying down a sail, for example, or putting a grass rope around the nose, or through the nose ring, of an ox or an ass. Then there was the wheel, another great agent of both traveling and taking up residence. The Kazaks say that their name comes from either a Turkish word meaning to wander, or a Mongol word for a wheeled cart.

It was around 3500 BCE that the wheel and the cart were harnessed up, and although at first the carts were heavy, with solid wheels, they allowed herders to move their shelter and supplies beyond the river valleys for extended periods, establishing summer and winter camps,

Bronze sun chariot with gold-mounted disk
(found in a peat-bog in Denmark, 10th century BCE)

and greatly expanding the number of animals they could maintain in a herd. The importance of the cart and the wagon is confirmed in early times by their routine presence in graves, to take the dead on their final journey.

Humans can walk just as far as horses, but they cannot go as fast across open ground. And they can't carry nearly as much. That's where horses first came into their own, with or without carts. Humans had used oxen and asses, and also dogs, to transport supplies for millennia; but the horse now gave them both speed and style.

There would have been no mistaking the advantages of a horse for transporting heavy tents and food and clothing and all the other things that people took about with them, including the tent hangings and small carvings, the little knickknacks and the musical instruments, which would have been strapped onto the back of a horse. Sometimes they would have dragged poles loaded with baggage. With horses, people could now move ten times further than formerly, and combat that worst of enemies, the weather. A traveling family would have been able to transport their belongings quickly, and relatively easily, across the plains and the steppes, and even into the mountains if the horses were carrying rather than pulling.

These migrations, which changed the face of the earth, would not have been possible—certainly not on the scale they took place—without horses. Many of these ancient peoples were nomadic; but this simply meant they stayed within a defined territory, following the seasons just as the Blackfoot followed the buffalo.

They were driven by both curiosity and a conviction that the world was bigger than they could picture. They created the global village, an imaginary community if ever there was one, and they provided new mobility for products and principles as well as people. Ironically, they made the world both larger *and* smaller. And more than paper and printing, more than the telephone and the television, more than radio and recording, and more than the Internet, the horse brought people together.

By the time of the Sumerian empire, in the north of what is now Iraq (in the third millennium BCE), and the Assyrian empire in the south (which began around 2000 BCE), horses were starting to take over from oxen and asses, and members of high society began to travel in horse-drawn chariots with spoked wheels.

This was traveling in style, and carts and chariots and carriages changed, both with new technologies—especially with respect to yokes and harnesses, wood and metal work, and road surfaces—and changing social conditions. Each culture developed its own breeds of horses—also dependent upon local conditions—and its own styles of coaches.

For a while, a cart with solid wheels was used by aristocrats in Mesopotamia, as it was in China and India (often with very large wheels to handle marshy or sandy ground); and when spoked wheels came into use, there were several varieties. Some were modeled after those of the Canaanites, light with four-spoke wheels. The Egyptians modified them into eight-spoke wheels, before settling for six spokes. Then the Greeks, fashion-conscious as always, returned to four spokes. Often the styles transcended national boundaries; but they usually also reflected regional or local fashions, balancing the aesthetic and expressive with the functional and practical. In Egypt and Greece a whole set of social as well as economic habits depended upon the use of chariots; just as in the eighteenth and nineteenth centuries in Europe and North America, as commerce increased and roads improved, the number of horse-drawn conveyances pulled by light draft or coach horses was both wonderfully diverse and—in social terms—absolutely precise.

To give a sense of the range during this period, here is a short list of popular coaches and carts: the barouche, the berlin, the break, the broughham, the buckboard, the buggy, the cabriolet, the calash (four-wheeled, one horse) and the caleche (two-wheeled, one horse), the chaise (or shay, in the United States), the charabanc, the clarence, the coupe, the dog cart (not pulled by dogs, but used to carry dogs to the hunt), the donkey cart (pulled by a pony), the governess cart, the hansom, the jogging cart, the stanhope gig, the ladies' stanhope, the landau and the landaulette (a kind of convertible landau), the phaeton (with variations such as the stanhope phaeton, the ladies' phaeton, and the spider phaeton—a souped-up ladies' phaeton for the men), the sulky, the surrey, the tandem, the tilbury and the trap . . . and those were just the basic types, with as many modifications as there are car models today.

But in the beginning, and indeed for thousands of years, there was a fundamental problem. There is one aspect of the early carts and chariots that is easily missed, and it has everything to do with the fact that wheeled vehicles were first pulled by oxen and then by horses.

"Pulled" is the operative word, for the rigging remained basically the same when horses took over: a yoke was attached in such a way that the animal pulled the wagon or cart by exerting pressure against its shoulders. This works well with an ox, which has high shoulders. But a horse is built differently; and even with a pad resting on its withers and held in place by a girth and a throat strap, a horse will still be pulling with its neck rather than its shoulders.

Which isn't where a horse is strongest. Horses can *push* much better than they can pull, since their power is in their hindquarters and they are most effective when they are leaning *into* the weight. Furthermore, the neck strap on the early yokes could rise up and press against the horse's windpipe. The exaggerated muscle development on the underside of the neck, represented in the ewe-necked posture that is evident in so much artwork of Egypt and Greece, would have only partly mitigated this. An additional strap was added, from the center of the neck strap between the front legs to the girth, but this did not really solve the problem.

Even though the throat-and-girth harness was neither comfortable for the horse nor an efficient use of horsepower, it worked—sort of. Horses managed to pull chariots for centuries this way. The trouble was that the chariots had to be kept light, and even then they were pulled by two—and often more—horses. Not bad for speed, but short on traction. Nevertheless, the throat-and-girth harness was universally used across the ancient West, while in China a modification of it seems to have been developed.

The term "pulling" is still used to describe what horses do in front of a cart. And "horsepower" identifies how fast and how far they go, and how much weight they pull. One horsepower was first defined, after experiments with draft horses, by James Watt, the eighteenth-century designer of the steam engine, as the amount of work required to pull a weight of 150 pounds out of a hole 220 feet deep (sometimes described as 33,000 foot-pounds) in one minute. A horse, when properly harnessed, can pull overloads of ten or fifteen times that for short periods, with pairs of horses developing over thirty horsepower.

"Properly harnessed," that is. Simple things sometimes slip by sophisticated people. Neither the Egyptians nor the

Greeks, nor the Etruscans nor the Persians, wise in so many ways, figured out that a horse wasn't nearly as efficient pulling as it would be pushing; and that a collar placed over its head would allow a horse to do just that, pushing against a padded ring that was itself harnessed directly to the load.

The Romans, with their engineering genius, seem to have understood this principle, though imperfectly. They developed a breast-strap harness with a swingle tree arrangement that went some way towards shifting the burden away from the neck, and they powered their four-horse/three-person chariot—the *quadriga*—this way. With a charioteer, a bowman, a helper, and sometimes a fourth person as outrider, it became the most elaborate chariot in the region, and incidentally provided the model for the modern armored car. The Mongols, too, are reported to have had a harness that went part way towards the shift from pulling to pushing, and they certainly had heavy carts to carry their tents and supplies and—after their raids—to haul away plunder.

It was the Scandinavians who developed the horse collar in medieval Europe. By the ninth century CE—on the evidence of burial sites and travelers' accounts—the collar was in general use with horses there for plowing the land, where the power required is much greater than in pulling a light cart or chariot. Insofar as this invention provided powerful locomotion for heavier carts in war, the plowshare was turned into a sword; but in fact the use of chariots of any sort in war had become very limited by this time. It took several more centuries for the plow horse to really come into its own, which it did when the medieval cavalry buckled under its own weight, and heavy war horses—of which there were lots by then—were out looking for work.

The horse collar and the stirrup are often cited as the most important inventions in the domestication of the horse. Both catch the element of contradiction that we

Two medieval farm workers with a harrow
(England, 14th century)

have seen time and again: the collar gave a horse the ability to push when it was pulling, and the stirrup allowed the rider to stand up while sitting down. They provided new power and mobility for horse and buggy and horse and rider. But it is a measure of the skill and strength of both horses and riders that some of the greatest achievements in chariotry and cavalry took place before either collars or stirrups were in common use.

Stirrups give the illusion of solid ground to riders who otherwise might not make it to the corner, and like the gun, they probably made people feel more powerful than they were. Many of the very best riders in the world did without stirrups, and later, many of the worst did with them. The Assyrians rode without stirrups, their hands free for shooting their bows and arrows, with their reins ingeniously attached to a collar around the horse's neck, weighted with a tassel to keep it in position. A quick tug on the collar and pressure with the legs would direct the horse wherever the rider wanted to go.

Stirrups also allow for subtle shifting of weight, not only to make the rider and horse more comfortable, but also to improve communication between them. Stirrups were—and still are—crudely used by some; but at their best, they can open up a new set of possibilities. One of these is to allow a rider to use a human being's handiest shock absorber, the ankle—much better than the butt—so that the looseness that good riders aspire to begins in the ankles and moves right up through the lower back and shoulders to the wrists and hands, where it is most crucial. The old saying about the ankle bone being connected to the wrist bone is especially true for a horseback rider. Using another metaphor, John Jennings notes that "a lot of false movement—like a knock in an engine—is caused by too much interference with the hands in an effort to 'collect' the horse from the front, instead of urging the horse up into the hands and then, with the utmost possible tact, asking the horse to find its own balance. The goal is to achieve that same balance and look of freedom under saddle that a horse sometimes assumes when free in a field."

Riders in India were using toe-stirrups—a looped rope that held the big toe—as early as 500 BCE, almost a thousand years before Attila the Hun, who is often credited with introducing stirrups to the rest of the world. More likely, stirrups went from India to China and then back across Asia to Europe, where they were in wide use by the time Charlemagne became emperor in 800 CE.

Whatever its provenance, the stirrup is a reminder of the ancient and highly developed equestrian tradition in India, often forgotten in the drama of the Mongol empires. The Indian technique of riding with toe-stirrups was classic horsemanship, on the edge between the ground and the air, keeping contact in a fine balance. And the tradition of elegant horsemanship remained strong on the subcontinent. In the early sixteenth century, when Babur —a descendant of Genghis Khan and Tamerlane—

A Mogul game of polo (drawing from ca. 1770)

founded India's Mogul dynasty, the miniature paintings that flourished at the Mogul court always depicted horses, no matter the subject, in tribute to their ancestors and the animal that brought them glory.

Stirrups had obvious advantages: they increased a rider's security in the saddle, they reduced fatigue, and they allowed for a wider range of riding styles that suited both heavily and lightly armed cavalry. Later, stirrups were a central feature of the working saddles of Spanish and then western design, where cowboys spent up to sixteen hours in the saddle and needed both comfort and support, not only during the long days but also for the strain that roping put on horse and rider.

≈

My grandfather, back in the 1880s, rode on a saddle that he had been given by Crop Eared Wolf. It was not much different from those that had been used by the Scythians around the time Homer was singing his songs, and probably by other nomadic tribes before that. The way of life of these great horse cultures, seemingly so distant in time and space, has a history stretching over 3,000 years right up to present-day Kazakstan, and their influence on contemporary horse traditions, East and West, ensures that they live on everywhere.

The saddle is one of the two basic items of tack for a riding horse; the other is the bridle. All saddles are designed to do the impossible, which is to fit together a human and a horse. It's like putting a round peg in a square hole; a person's bottom and a pony's back are not built the same way.

There are two ways of dealing with this. One is the sailor's way: use the wind blowing in one direction to move a boat in another, and hold on. The other is the Shaker's way: make a comfortable chair. Saddles combine both; they are a rider's seat and sail, all in one.

The first saddles weren't saddles at all—they were blankets. That did the trick for a couple of thousand years; but slowly, as people designed harnesses (and later collars), they would have become aware of ways of redirecting weight and reducing wear on the horse, and then on the rider.

The ancient Scythian saddle had a felt saddlecloth, often elegantly embroidered, as we know from examples found in frozen tombs in Siberia where horses and riders, complete with all the tack and trimmings, were strangled and buried with the nobles. The cloth would probably be used as a blanket at night. The saddle itself was of leather and felt, with two cushions stuffed with hair—from local animals like the reindeer—joined together with straps or a strip of leather. The cushions were placed on either side of the horse's spine, to distribute the weight of the rider and keep it off the withers and the backbone.

That same saddle, padded in essentially the same way, eventually found its way around the world. The gauchos—or cowboys—of Argentina used a saddle almost exactly like that used by the Scythians, and the Blackfoot and other plains Indian tribes took it up from the Spanish, using buffalo, elk, or antelope hide and buffalo or deer hair as stuffing, and typically decorated with porcupine-quill beadwork. The modern jumping saddle is still very close in design to those earliest saddles, and has provided a model for general-purpose saddles in wide currency, especially for folks who ride forward so that their weight is behind the horse's withers rather than in the middle of his back (which is the weakest part of the horse from an engineering standpoint). On this saddle, the rider is more a sailor than a sitter, trying to make sure the wind doesn't spill out of the sail.

The challenge for every rider is to draw on the power in the horse's hindquarters with the legs and seat, while making sure it doesn't escape out the front through the hands. The key is balance, in every sense, with constant attention to riffles and shifts. Fighting with the wind, or the horse, will never work.

Horses and the wind have always been fellow travelers. The word we use for saddles and stirrups and bridles and bits is tack, a latter-day descendant of nautical tackle. And the ways in which a rider relates to a horse are remarkably similar to the ways in which a sailor relates to the wind: by indirection—and always on the edge.

The other type of saddle has an honorable place in the history of riding, and is also of ancient heritage. It had a frame or "tree," and provided a stable seat. The first saddle built on this principle seems to have been developed by the Sarmatians, eastern neighbors of the Scythians, probably first of all for the heavy war lances they used instead of spears and arrows. This saddle allowed the rider to withstand considerable impact, and it was adopted by many in the centuries to follow. The Arab saddle was a variant, built high at front with a wide cantle behind to protect the kidneys. And it had leather girths, sometimes with breast and haunch straps, just like the Scythian saddle. The Blackfoot, on the other hand, used a saddle like this for women, old folks, and children, and for packing buffalo meat and other supplies. It had wooden sideboards and high cantle and pommel, made either of cottonwood or—in what was known as the prairie chicken snare saddle—with elk or deer antlers.

The sidesaddle, first mentioned in the fourteenth century CE, was initially little more than a stuffed seat allowing a lady to sit sideways, her feet resting on a small platform; but by the sixteenth century a pommel over which a rider could hook her knee gave some security, and an opportunity to look where she was going. Later modifications included a balance strap and a "leaping head" pommel that curved over the rider's thigh.

Whatever the design, the fundamentals of a good saddle are to put the rider in a balanced position so that he or she can influence the horse through pressure with the legs, and so that the weight of the rider does not rest on the loins of the horse. A good saddle, be it for herding reindeer or raiding the enemy, for jumping or dressage, needs to put the rider's legs directly underneath.

John Jennings picks up the theme, drawing on his wide experience: "You should be able to visualize the horse being removed and the rider out on the ground, still in perfect balance, with the knees bent and the back slightly arched so that there is a line straight down from the back of the shoulders to the back of the seat to the back of the heels. Good cowboy working saddles used to put the rider in this position, so that the rider could influence the horse mostly with legs and a shift of balance. Now a lot of the western saddles put the rider in the armchair position, with legs unable to do a damn thing and the weight on the horse's loins."

Changing from dressage to jumping, then, all a rider has to do is to shorten the stirrups and lean forward, taking the weight off the horse's back end but maintaining the same center of gravity by shifting the seat back as the body goes forward.

The better the rider the more the legs are used, and the less the hands. This is where the horse and rider each have to give a little. A horse instinctively pushes against pressure —that's the whole point about "pulling" and horsepower —and needs to learn to yield to the leg. The rider, for his or her part, needs to restrain the use of hands, which also doesn't come naturally because we use our hands to do so much that matters to us.

Which is where bridles and bits come into the picture. Throughout the ages, two main styles of riding emerged. One was fixed firmly in a saddle, controlling the horse by a bridle and a bit in the mouth; the other involved contact with the horse through shifts of weight and pressure on the nose.

Both had their purpose and place—and every great horse culture came up with a style that combined elements of each, and a compromise between them has dominated European and American riding for the past century.

The oldest technique of control was the nose ring, used on oxen before horses. And the first bridle would have been a strip of woven grass wound around the nose, with a rope around the lower jaw added sometime later. (This type of bridle was revived by the Blackfoot, in what became known as a "war bridle.") At some point a set of reins was passed through the nose ring, or around the nose and up round the neck so that a rider—or someone riding in a cart behind— had a way of sending signals to the front end of the horse, where steering and braking are controlled.

There are many ways of controlling a horse—some of which should never be put in writing—but the head is where the action is. That's why, in the old days, even supposedly rough-and-tough cowboys never fooled around up front. That was sacred ground: a horse's head belonged to the horse, and bronco-busters—called *domadores* in Argentina and *amansadores* in Mexico—could be fired for abusing a horse's head or shoulders. In fact, horse-breakers were much more often horse-gentlers; their job was to get a horse to accept a saddle and to stand still. Then it was over to the rider for training, and no cowboy wanted to work with a horse that was afraid of humans.

A horse has a big nose, so it's natural that the nose was the first thing to be used for steering and braking. Then came the mouth, probably soon after. For 5,000 years, there have been arguments about which works best. But since the mouth and the nose are not far apart in a horse, neither could expect to be left out of the action for long. Most bridles and bits bring some pressure on both.

Of course, just as many exceptional riders throughout history have worked without saddles and stirrups, so have they also done without bits and even bridles. There is a tradition of riding without bits long after they were widely available, and in North Africa riders sometimes controlled their horses with a light switch between the ears, the way some people still manage donkeys.

*Snaffle decorated with two winged ibex
(from Iran, 8th to 7th century BCE)*

But just as some form of bridle seems to go back to the beginning, when humans first domesticated horses, so quite certainly does the bit; we have evidence from Dereivka, the Copper Age village in Ukraine where the "cult stallion" was found. There are two basic types of bit, the snaffle and the curb. The snaffle, which has been around for about 6,000 years, acts on the tongue and the edges of the mouth, with a mouthpiece that slips inside the mouth and comes to rest in the space between the front and back teeth. Realizing that horses have that space in the gum on the lower jaw—called a bar—on which a piece of bone or metal could rest was one of humanity's great discoveries. It had evolved to provide horses with a kind of holding pocket, a mouth pouch, for grasses, leaves, and twigs before the serious chewing began, and it was tailor-made for bits.

As horses became larger, and as the feeding began to include high-energy grains, the need for greater steering and braking mechanisms became apparent, and so the snaffle bit was "jointed" in the middle to squeeze the face, an action that was sometimes intensified with rings or cheeks added to the ends of the mouthpiece. Most snaffles are now jointed, and control is exercised with reins attached to the rings at the corner of the mouthpiece.

The curb was a later invention, probably introduced by the Celts in the fourth century BCE; it is mentioned by Xenophon a little later. Its mouthpiece is usually similar to a snaffle's, but it creates extra leverage by attaching a cheekpiece and adding a shank or curb chain below the mouthpiece to create pressure at the top of the head or on the lower jaw. For fifteen hundred years, this was the bit that most people used, and—given the opinionated habits of horse people—folks would scoff at those who rode with a snaffle rather than a curb. But recently, there has been a general return to the snaffle, often with a noseband.

After the snaffle and the curb, there have been no further inventions when it comes to bits. Both allow for a

wide range of riding techniques, and both have been modified in all sorts of ways to suit different riding styles. Living
in open country, the Scythians—like the plains Indians—
developed a style of riding that suited hunting and raiding
with bows and arrows; they rode fast, with a snaffle bit and
a loose rein leaving both hands free, and they crouched forward in the saddle much like jockeys or show jumpers.

An alternative style, adopted by the ancient Persians
and Greeks, was more straight-up, the horse collected with
a bit that raised up his head (by pulling upwards on the
corner of the lips) and encouraged his hindquarters under
the body.

Then again, a cowboy sitting tall in the saddle to rope
a steer might ride on a well-trained horse without any bit
at all. The apparently archetypal distinction between the
free and easy riding style of the "barbarian" and the con-
tained and collected form of the "civilized" rider is nothing of the sort. Both were suited to the circumstances, and
both were the product of sound equestrian theory.

And even obvious distinctions can be deceptive. My
grandfather's bridle, called a hackamore, didn't have a bit;
in that sense it was like the Blackfoot bridle of his friend
Crop Eared Wolf. But the two bridles operated on quite

different principles. My grandfather's bridle focused on the horse's nose; Crop Eared Wolf's bridle on the mouth.

The Blackfoot bridle was often called a war bridle because it was used in battle, though the Blackfoot also used it in the buffalo hunt, as well as in everyday travel. It was made of single strand or braided rawhide, and consisted of a single length of rope with a *honda* (a small loop) at one end, passed around the horse's neck with two half hitches taken in the rope before it was placed in the horse's mouth and tightened around his lower jaw. The free end of the rope was then brought up around the other side of the horse's neck and through the honda. For the rider, the end with the honda served as one rein, the other end as the second rein. The rest of the rope, which might be as long as thirty feet, was coiled and tucked into his belt for use as a lariat to lasso horses or cattle—or, if the rider was thrown, as a way of keeping hold of the horse.

There were a number of other tricks of the trade, as there always are when humans and horses get together, like adding a third hitch in the mouthpiece for a hard-to-control horse (the rawhide hitches would swell in the horse's mouth). A single half hitch was used by the

Blackfoot for racehorses; while on parade a long loop of the bridle rope—or sometimes a scalp—was left hanging under the horse's jaw to move and strike the horse's nose if he didn't keep his head up.

The hackamore that my grandfather used was a bridle of ancient origin—the word comes from the Arabic *hakma* by way of the Spanish *jáquima*—and consisted of a heavy braided rawhide noseband (called a *bosal*) with a large knot (called the heel knot) that lay under the horse's chin, held in place by a light headstall placed over the horse's ears, with a band across the brow to hold it in place. A relatively heavy rope, often made of hair from the horse's mane or of cotton, was tied to the heel knot with a series of wraps— the number of which determined how much pressure could be applied by the rider—and carried on up to act as reins, with the bridle balanced by the large knot and the rope reins on the one hand, and the substantial nosepiece on the other. A throatlatch—a light rope around the throat and behind the ears—was usually added to prevent the heel knot from bumping into the lower jaw.

The result was—and still is—a system in which it is pressure on the nose, rather than the mouth, that provides direction to the horse. It is the apotheosis of the "nose" school of riding, part of a tradition that produced horses and riders both for combat and for working with cattle and bulls at full speed, directed by a floating rein and the shift of the rider's body. Not surprisingly, given the need for quick turns and fast starts in polo, hackamores have also been used to train polo ponies.

The hackamore requires, and rewards, delicate hands and a good sense of how to shift weight to control the horse; but the leverage *is* significant, and since the nose is a sensitive part of a horse it needs a rider with knowledge and experience to be successful. A curb bit is often added, with a high port (or inverted U) in the mouthpiece to allow more room for the tongue and to dampen the pressure of the mouthpiece. It also offers the possibility of applying great pressure on the roof of the mouth; but the experienced western rider using this rig with subtlety rather than strength inflicts far less pain on a horse than many of those in the European stable salons, who scorn it as barbaric, associating it with the great but sometimes harsh tradition of Spanish equitation.

Vaquero horse tamers in the 1880s brought the hackamore to the West, carrying on a tradition that had come to them from colonial Spain, and before that from seven centuries of Moorish rule in the Iberian peninsula. One observer, writing in 1884 from a ranch near Milk River, Alberta, in Crop Eared Wolf's homeland, described how the vaqueros would catch the horses "by the front foot and by a twist throw them, and while they were down put on the hackamore and blindfold them, then let them up. A blinded horse will usually stand when held without too much fuss till the saddle is on. . . . The hackamore is a braided rawhide halter with the headstall fairly close fitting and the nosepiece adjustable so that pulling down on the shanks smothers a horse down, cutting off his wind and making him possible to control."

The vaqueros—their Portuguese name was *vaqueiros* —were the cowboys of the *sertao*, the dry plains of the northeast of Brazil as well as of northern Mexico and the Spanish-American Southwest. Some of them ended up in the North, running herds right up into the Blackfoot territory and the country where Big Bird came out of the hills. Way down south, on the pampas of the Rio de la Plata in Argentina—perhaps the world's richest natural grazing land—and the Rio Grande do Sul of southern Brazil, it was the legendary gauchos who followed the herds, while *llaneros* in Venezuela and *huasos* in Chile extended the Spanish tradition of riding throughout the Americas. But like the hackamore and the horse itself, these traditions ultimately came from far and wide.

＊

Some riding styles, past and present, are not gentle, and some of the bits, ironically during the age of chivalry, were frightening. Still, medieval knights probably did less damage to their horses than some modern riders, because they rode by neck reining, just like the riders who use a hackamore.

Some say that worrying about the horse was a luxury a man of war could not afford. But like cowboys, warriors of ancient and medieval times couldn't afford *not* to look after their horses either, even when they had several to spare, for their survival depended on them. That had been the case from the earliest days, and for millennia humans have paid tribute to their favorite horses in tales and poems, in paintings and carvings, and in funeral cere-monies and burial mounds.

Throughout history, anyone who could tame a horse and train a rider was also celebrated in story and song, and paid a premium. From the beginning, there would have been a horse whisperer for every horse whipper. And the results would have shown. Many of the people in these cultures knew a lot more about horses, and depended on them much more, than we do. They would have recognized success, and built upon it. The transformation in training methods achieved by Ray Hunt and Buck Brannaman and Monty Roberts and others in America, like the transformation achieved earlier in Europe by men like the Italian Federico Caprilli (often considered the "father of modern riding") and Alois Podhajsky (the director of the Spanish Riding School in Vienna from 1936 to 1965) should remind us that people *do* pay attention. And the titles of their books should tell us something about their principles, from Podhajsky's *My Horses, My Teachers* to Hunt's *Think Harmony with Horses*. Trainers have been trying new methods, and relearning old ones, since the beginning of time.

It is worth remembering that just as the warlike nomads shaped ancient horse culture, it was the cavalry tradition—the preeminent method of war for over two thousand years—that schooled many of the greatest riders of the twentieth century, and from which much of today's equestrian understanding derives. Form and function came together, after the artifices of the previous centuries, in a shift in focus to the natural movement of the horse and its natural abilities, with riding techniques that emphasized a new kind of collaboration between horse and rider. One of the wonderful ironies of this change is that it emerged not out of some pastoral romanticism, but out of the great Italian military schools at Tor di Quinto and Pinerolo, and their followers in the Polish riding academies. And it was from these and other cavalry schools that some of the finest coaches took lessons home to their own communities—trainers like Harry Chamberlin, who spent his career in the United States Cavalry, put together its core instruction manual on horsemastership, and authored the classic *Riding and Schooling Horses* (1935); Vladimir Littauer, who served in the Russian Imperial Cavalry and wrote *Commonsense Horsemanship* (1951); and the British equestrian Henry Wynmalen, author of *The Horse in Action* (1954).

Chapter 4

MAKING TROUBLE

Horses in War

There are many famous horses in history. Along with racehorses like Eclipse and Seabiscuit and Secretariat and Northern Dancer, some of them are well known for founding a family—like the Darley Arabian, one of the fathers of the English Thoroughbreds, and Justin Morgan, of the Morgan breed. Or for being mythical or fictional favorites—like Pegasus and Black Beauty and My Friend Flicka. Or for carrying famous men in war—like

Bucephalus (the horse of Alexander the Great) or Ouskob the Torrent (Muhammad's horse) or Nelson (George Washington's) or Marengo (Napoleon's) or Bel Argent (Toussaint L'Ouverture's).

But the most famous horse of all, in the most famous war of all, had no name at all. In fact, he wasn't even a horse.

The Trojan Horse was made of wood, and ended the ten-year-long assault of Troy. In Homer's *Odyssey*, Odysseus tells about the trick—his idea, he claims—that the Greeks played on the Trojans. They had a large replica built of a horse, hid some Greek soldiers inside, and then sailed away from Troy as though they were giving up their siege of the heavily fortified city. When the Trojans—like

Napoleon Crossing the Alps (Jacques Louis David, 1801)

most of us unable to resist the appeal of a remarkable horse—took the wooden horse in, the Greek soldiers rushed out at night and conquered the city.

The Trojan Horse was the ultimate wartime Big Lie. Maybe one of the reasons the fraud worked is that the Trojans, like all good horsemen, knew that horses do not lie. Which they don't! When Jonathan Swift had his traveler Gulliver visit the land of the horses—whom he called Houyhnhnms, after the whinnying sound they made—he said that they found it impossible "to say the thing that was not." Unlike humans, whom the horses called Yahoos.

But the Trojan Horse was a force for change, and in that sense, it was like all horses throughout history. One of the things horses changed was the way humans waged war. In fact, horses really invented war as we know it.

"People often say that force is no argument," said Oscar Wilde. "But that depends on what you are trying to prove." Horses helped prove that humans could destroy each other. And then go and get more horses in order to do more damage elsewhere. Not only did horses invent war; they started the arms race.

In the beginning, though, they just simplified the odds. If you had horses, you won. End of story. Horses were the ancient—and medieval—equivalent of planes and tanks, and horsemen, recognizing the advantage they had, bore down on their enemies, rained down arrows and spears on them, and then raced off. This was the basic principle of both cavalry and chariotry. Horses gave warriors both superior height and superior speed, a combination that will almost always overwhelm an opponent, certainly in open combat and often with very few casualties to the winning force. To this day, the police and the army ride horses to supervise the streets and control the crowds. In the old days, anyone who did not have horses of good quality, and the skill and experience to use them, was a sitting duck against an army of riders (at least until the crossbow and later the rifle evened the odds a bit). But even then, horses still ruled.

The earliest horsemen are usually given the less complimentary name of barbaric hordes, though modern military commanders would probably love to have had some Huns or Scythians on their side, with their lightning raids and their deadly retaliation against anyone who trespassed on their territory or disturbed their tombs (which were the only permanent homes they knew). The word "cavalry" survives in the lexicon of the mechanized warfare of the last hundred years, a tribute to the horses that gave war its grim character and horse warriors a deadly advantage.

✐

For several thousand years, horses were the single most important instrument of war. All kinds of horses. First it was fast horses, for the raids and retaliations. Then it was extra-strong horses, for the war wagons and chariots that played a major part in battle from about 2000 BCE, especially in the wars that took place between relatively settled societies, and for nearly a thousand years chariot warfare remained the dominant mode. Chariots had their limitations, especially if the terrain was uneven; but they also had enormous shock value. Then it was back to fast horses, when highly trained and organized cavalry forces became more common in the first millennium BCE.

Not surprisingly, given the history of horses and humans, it was from Asia that chariots first clattered and crashed into the Western world. The Hyksos took control of the Nile Delta in the eighteenth century BCE with chariot warfare; one description has the chariots coming like arrows shot from a bow, horses' hooves thundering past the frontier posts day and night. It may have been a more measured takeover; but it certainly brought much of the horse culture of Asia into the Middle East and North Africa. Horses were still relatively scarce in the region at that time. In Assyria, for example, a horse was worth thirty slaves or five hundred sheep. But soon, as with most military toys, everybody wanted some of those horses, and this led to raids on neighboring communities, especially in Syria, where the Mittanians—of Indo-Aryan ancestry—had taken up residence, and in Canaan, where light chariots were already in use from the beginning of the second millennium BCE. The first mention of horses in the Bible (in Genesis 47) is of Joseph receiving horses and other livestock from the lands of Egypt and Canaan, about 1700 BCE. It was in this region, too, that the Hittite horsemaster Kikkuli wrote his famous horse-training manual.

By 1600 BCE, the Egyptians—having finally thrown out the invading Hyksos—had secured some fine chariot horses, and within relatively short order the great Egyptian military pharaoh Tuthmose III had established a standing army, organized into divisions of 5,000 men, with chariotry and infantry, and he had fought the first chariot battle of which we have an account, at Megiddo in Syria, in 1469 BCE against allies of the Hyksos. John Keegan calls this "the first battle in history," in the sense that we know with fair certainty when and where and who and what happened (though that confines history to written sources, which is a severe limitation). In any case, it signaled an important moment for Egypt, one in which horses were crucial. True to form, the Egyptians began to commemorate them in paintings that belong with those of the Ice Age cave dwellers for giving us a sense of the horses' spiritual as well as physical presence.

This seems to have bothered the prophets of Israel, even though their people were using Egyptian horses to defend themselves against the invading Assyrians. Isaiah, among others, railed against this: "Woe to them that go down to Egypt for help, and stay on horses, and trust in chariots. . . . The Egyptians are men and not God, and their horses flesh and not spirit." But in an ancient version of Cromwell's maxim—"Praise God and keep your powder dry"—the Israelites continued to call on both God and the Egyptians for help. This enabled them to keep the Assyrians more or less at bay, achieving victories such as the one over the notorious Sennacherib, celebrated by Byron in a famous poem (inspired by another passage in Isaiah):

The Assyrian came down like the wolf on the fold,
And his cohorts were gleaming in purple and gold;
And the sheen of their spears was like stars on the sea,
When the blue wave rolls nightly on deep Galilee.

A chariot attack must have been an awesome sight, and the sound too must have been overwhelming. Chariots were a formidable offensive weapon, but in the midst of a battle, with horses only partly under control, there must have been some fearsome pileups. Also, horses were vulnerable to the equestrian equivalent of anti-aircraft fire—arrows shot and spears thrown by infantry. And since most of the horses in those early centuries of chariotry and cavalry were relatively small—pony-size, in fact—they could not carry armor thick enough to withstand heavy attack.

Partly because of this vulnerability, chariots came increasingly to be used as troop carriers—sort of like armored personnel vehicles—as often as they were deployed as weapons of attack. In the *Iliad*, chariots taxied the warriors to the fighting ground. In other accounts of the time, they carried back the spoils of war. By the time Homer wrote about the Trojan War at the beginning of the first millennium BCE, cavalry was taking over; and henceforth, until the end of the Roman Empire in the fifth century CE, chariots were mostly used to transport troops—and for military shows, which often took the form of races like the one Homer describes in Book 23 of the *Iliad*. Organized by Achilles to commemorate the death of his friend Patroclus at the hands of Hector, tamer of horses, it is one of the most vivid descriptions of conflict in the entire epic.

～

There were many ways of getting horses—other than trading for them. Raids and annual tributes were the most common, and for a powerful country an obvious way of adding to the arsenal (and diminishing that of others). The Persians, like most imperial powers of the time, levied a horse tax against those they conquered; Cappadocia alone had to provide them with 1,500 horses a year, while Cilicia (well known for its horse breeding) was required to give 360 white horses annually.

But honest trading—or at least horse trading—still counted for something, and there were some formidable stables. One nonroyal owner in Babylon, according to Herodotus, had over 16,000 mares and 800 stallions. And horse breeders and traders were coming into their own to handle the demand. Some regions, such as Syria, were renowned for the superior quality and quantity of their horses, and so everyone who was anyone in the military world of that time fought in and over Syria—from the Mittanians, Hittites, Egyptians, and Assyrians, to the Armenians, Persians, and Macedonians.

Syria's history of horses is a long and distinguished one, stretching from at least the eighteenth century BCE to the eighteenth century CE, when the Darley Arabian was purchased at Aleppo, smuggled out of the country in violation of an Ottoman prohibition against exporting purebred Arabs, and brought to England to extend a tradition of horse breeding begun by Charles II. The Darley Arabian is one of the three foundation stallions of what became known as the Thoroughbred line. The others were the Byerley Turk—said to have been a Captain Byerley's charger in William of Orange's campaign in Ireland in the late seventeenth century—and the Godolphin Barb, who was discovered by a shrewd horse trader, pulling a water-cart in Paris around 1728. He had been given to Louis XV by the Bey of Tunis, but wasn't to the king's liking, and so was sold and ended up on the streets. The Darley Arabian was the great-great-grandsire of Eclipse, one of the most famous racehorses of all time, born in 1764 during an eclipse of the sun (and dying of colic in 1789). In turn, Eclipse was the grandsire of over a hundred winners of the Epsom Derby, England's greatest flat race.

Trade in horses was not without its restrictions. This was partly for security reasons—to maintain military advantage—and partly to preserve the purity of certain breeds. In both cases, as usual, pride and prejudice played their part. At one time, many breeders of Arab horses believed—wrongly—that an Arab sire who had mated with a non-Arab mare was forever compromised, and that

Arab Thoroughbred (Alfred Dedreux, ca. 1846)

his future progeny, even by a purebred Arab mare, would be tainted. And vice versa. These breeders were not alone in their obsession with purity. In many places, mixing was as prohibited for people as it was for horses.

Such prejudices against "foreign" blood were an early version of race-based immigration policies, and strict reference to bloodlines became part of the culture of horses. It still is, and has wide currency in the various horse breeding associations around the world, who hold high their stud books and breeding records.

But ironically, *mixed* heritages have produced some of our greatest horses, as is evident from the history of horse breeding in general, and the curiously named Thoroughbred lineage in particular. For thousands of years, the breeding of pure lines has been countered by a commitment to hybrids, with one supposed "breed" being crossed with other stock to reinforce and then replicate certain characteristics. There are economic as well as social reasons for each of these approaches, and they protect different interests; but science often gets short shrift.

And maybe it should. At the end of the day, horse breeding—like many things having to do with horses—is as much an art as it is a science. For millennia, horses have been fashioned according to human needs and desires, as well as environmental conditions—nurture and nature. And just as riding was a stylization of social and psychological attitudes as well as of scientific knowledge of tack and equestrian techniques, so breeding preferences reflected larger preoccupations. Some of them were quite practical, like breeding for chariot or cavalry purposes, or for draft and carriage. But others were bound into political ambitions. For instance, after the Second World War the French, with their concern for national standards in language and culture, promoted the development of a single breed of saddle horse. The Germans, on the other hand, now shying away from national types and committed to local cultural differences, produced an astonishing range of regional breeds, including the Mecklenburg, Oldenburg, Hanoverian, Westphalian, Hessian, Württemberg, and the Bavarian Warmblood.

For several thousand years much of the breeding of horses for speed or size or stamina was driven by the demands of war. Horses were part of a country's war arsenal, and strict embargoes—often on pain of death—against selling horses to the enemy were common. In the Middle Ages, Spain, France, and England all banned the export of horses, and England even banned exports to Scotland under the Tudors. And while such bans were often broken, they give us a sense of the importance of horses in those societies.

Horse parades, in all cultures, provided an opportunity for countries to show off their military equipment; they were an early version of those pompous parades of war machinery that have been popular in both autocratic regimes and democracies for at least a hundred years, impressing folks on the home front and hopefully terrorizing the other side. And they find another expression in the statues and monuments of great (or not so great) leaders on horseback that punctuate parks and plazas around the world.

As chariots and other drawn conveyances became more widely used in the second millennium BCE, there was a need for larger horses to pull them, especially in the years before an effective harness was designed. And so everyone went looking for such horses.

In ancient China, where chariots were developed early and large horses had come to be at a premium, the legendary horses of Ferghana, well fed and sixteen hands high, were greatly prized. Around 100 BCE, the emperor Wu-ti initiated a major raid to that far western territory to bring back horses. His soldiers secured 3,000 of them, but only the 50 strongest survived the 2,000-mile trek back.

During the Middle Ages, horses were bred for size to carry the knights in all their armor, and to give greater force to the impact of their lances; and then, when the advent of firearms forced the cavalry once more onto smaller, swifter horses, the "great horses" of the knights morphed into a civilian role and became the foundation of much of Europe's modern draft and show stock. Many of the draft horses that we now think of as bred for peaceful purposes —like the Percherons and the Belgians—began their careers as war horses, and only later turned to farm work, and pulling canal barges, and hauling heavy loads before the railroad came along. The Suffolk is the only common draft breed specifically raised for the farm.

❧

Breeding for particular purposes, and designing appropriate tack, is of perennial importance when it comes to horses. But the most important element has always been training. Not surprisingly, all the early writings we have on horses are directed towards preparing for war, just as much of the modern development in equitation came out of cavalry schools. But sports and entertainment also played their part; after the chariot became obsolete in war, the Romans took the idea of an arena dedicated to horseracing—the hippodrome—from the Greeks, and built elaborate "circuses," the largest of which, the Circus Maximus in Rome, is said to have seated 200,000 spectators. This was big entertainment, often brutal and bloody, and big business. And it created a cohort of drivers—many of them slaves or working-class men—who were exceptionally gifted.

Other equestrian sports, like flat racing and games on horseback such as polo and *buzkashi*, are also ancient. Buzkashi, in which a goat or calf skin is filled with sand, soaked in water overnight, and fought over by teams from ten to as many as a thousand riders, has been played in central Asia since time immemorial. It goes back to the Scythians—the word means "to steal a goat"—and it requires extraordinary equestrian abilities and a cavalier disregard of the risks involved.

Hunting—the archetypal sport with horses—had an additional advantage as a training ground for armed conflict, since it addressed a fundamental issue for a mounted warrior, and indeed for any rider at work or play—a horse's natural instinct to run away from things, rather than right at them. A chariot horse, no less than a cavalry mount or a show jumper, had to be trained to go against the grain. Hunting was an obvious—and since war was the touchstone which people understood—appropriately dangerous way of putting this to the test. Many of the great military commanders in ancient times boasted of their hunting prowess, like Tiglath Pileser I of Assyria, who lived around 1100 BCE and said that he had killed eight hundred lions from his chariot. Many of the images from this period show encounters between chariots and lions, as though to underline that the natural order has been reversed.

Hunting with horses was but one of several human practices that contradicted their natural behavior (beginning with riding and driving). Letting someone onto your back—when your deepest instincts tell you that's where lions land—does not come naturally to a horse; just like someone holding onto you from behind—like wolves do when they want to drag you down—doesn't. And certainly not going on the attack. The Bible, in one of its rare references to horses (in Job 39), describes the challenge in a way that does justice to the courage involved:

He paweth in the valley, and rejoiceth in his strength;
he goeth on to meet the armed men. He mocketh at
fear, and is not afrighted; neither turneth he back from
the sword. The quiver rattleth against him, the glitter-
ing spear and the shield. He swalloweth the ground
with fierceness and rage; neither believeth he that it is
the sound of the trumpet. He saith among the trum-
pets, Ha, ha; and he smelleth the battle afar off, the
thunder of the captains, and the shouting.

Breeding counts for something here. Knowledge of
horse training matters, too. Because Xenophon had served
as a mercenary in a campaign led by Cyrus the Younger to
overthrow the Persian leader Artaxerxes II, much of his
celebrated commentary on the care and training of horses
reflects what he had learned about Persian equestrian
methods, which were renowned at the time. This was long
after the Persians had defeated the Medes (in 550 BCE)
and taken over their legendary cavalry, then considered
the best in the world. The Persians subsequently established a tradition of riding that included everyone of every
rank. This was a significant social change, though not one
to worry the aristocrats; horses were still synonymous

with status, and so Persian nobles were now instructed to travel on horseback, never on foot, no matter how short the distance. (This is the origin, perhaps, of our own tradition of automobile transportation for dignitaries whenever they need to go a few steps down the road.)

But until riding replaced driving in prestige and power in a culture, as it had for the Persians, those high in the hierarchy usually listened to their advisors and remained in the relative safety of the chariot—their ancient limousines. This was sensible for both social and strategic purposes, and in war it was standard, since many of the rulers didn't know how to ride very well, and most of the battles were fought on level ground anyway—where chariots rolled along relatively smoothly.

꙳

Horses drawing chariots were often armored with a woven-hair or leather pad across their backs, and the standard account has it that battle engagement involved chariot charges. But a big question mark is in order here.

As historians who know about horses have pointed out, the clashes that would have been an inevitable—and indeed intentional—part of any chariot (or cavalry) charge would have been devastating for the horses. So why would any serious warrior, unless absolutely required, indulge in them? Horses were too valuable to be put at such risk, and given the numbers of horses used to pull chariots, the losses could have been catastrophic. Since the chariots were relatively lightweight, designed for speed on the straight and for swift turns, mashing them up in a crash would be like putting a wide receiver up against a tackle or a guard in a scrimmage. Also, rear-end collisions would have been unavoidable, and the infantry that presumably followed a horse charge would not make much progress over the thrashing hooves.

And finally, for the soldier riding "shotgun" with the driver to be able to fire an arrow or throw a javelin with any accuracy during a charge, the chariots would have to be going at one of two speeds: a full gallop, or a slow canter. Only at these couple of gaits does a horse move with a minimum up-and-down motion; but both of them entail obvious hazards. Going flat out at a full gallop, a chariot could not turn quickly and avoid a collision. And at a slow canter, it would become an easy target.

By the seventh century BCE, the limitations of chariots on the front line and the challenges of uneven terrain meant that cavalry was coming into wider use in the Near and Middle East, giving an army great mobility and force. Ben Hur aside—and the elegant figure of a charioteer did continue to have a strong hold on visual artists and their princely patrons for a long time—some of our greatest stories of horses in war involve riders, not drivers.

It was on horseback that warriors, from the Scythians to the Huns, from Alexander the Great to Genghis Khan, and from the Muslim colonizers and the Christian crusaders to the Spanish conquistadors and the Indians of the plains, conquered and controlled and contested empires and caught the imagination of the world. The stories of their campaigns are among the greatest in the history of war and shaped both military strategies and equestrian skills right up to the present. They also provided a foundation for the care and training of horses that is still practiced today. Modern methods of warfare, in the air with jet fighters as well as on the ground with tank battalions, owe much to horse cavalry; and the great cavalry regiments— like Alexander's Macedonian Companion Cavalry or the Mongolian horsemen of Genghis Khan—employed tactics which overwhelmed their enemies and have astonished military experts ever since.

Cavalry figured prominently in many of the campaigns during the Persian battles with Greece, and then in the interminable fights between the Greek states during the Peloponnesian Wars in the fifth century BCE. Greece did not have a great horse tradition at this time, and Xenophon wrote his treatise to some extent in order to improve the Athenian cavalry. These were violent times, and a good cavalry—along with well-nourished baggage beasts—was becoming crucial. Nobody would demonstrate this more decisively than Alexander the Great.

Alexander of Macedonia was one of the first great horse warriors we know a good deal about. And he was one of the most famous horse whisperers.

A horse had been brought by a horse dealer from Thessaly to sell to Philip, who was the leader of the Macedonians at the time. The local people had named him Bucephalus after the brand on his backside in the shape of an ox-head, a *boukephalus*.

The year was 344 BCE, and even back then horse traders had a dicey reputation. The horse looked splendid when he moved out; but he turned out to be vicious when anybody closed in on him. Philip was about to send horse and horse trader packing; but his son Alexander, who was only twelve at the time, asked if he could try to gentle the horse. Alexander must have been one of those youngsters who took up a halter before he took up a hairbrush, or perhaps he first used his hairbrush on a horse. In any event, he understood things that the horse trader—and perhaps even the horse—didn't.

Alexander noticed that Bucephalus shied when he saw his own shadow move, and so he turned the stallion to face the sun. Bucephalus stood quiet; the boy jumped on his back—and into history.

Bucephalus helped Alexander the Great establish the largest empire the world had ever known, stretching 17,000 miles from Alexandria to Ferghana and from Macedonia to India. Although he was brought from the plains of Thessaly, Bucephalus's lineage was probably either Akhal-Teke— bred in the Akhal valley, an oasis in the middle of the Karakun desert in central Asia, its horses renowned for being able to go for up to three days without water—or

Alexander and Bucephalus
(Pompeii, Italy, ca. 1st century CE)

possibly from Ferghana. He took Alexander on campaigns from regions where the temperatures reached 120 degrees Fahrenheit, to the ice and snow of the Hindu Kush, traveling across grassland and marshland, through desert and monsoon. Bucephalus died—legend has it at the age of thirty—after Alexander's final battle at the River Hydaspes in the Punjab, and Alexander named a city after him.

When Alexander came to power—on the assassination of his father Philip in 336 BCE—he inherited the dangerously confused relations in the region, and a strong army of 400 light horse scouts and over 3,300 heavy horse cavalry armed with an almost twenty-foot-long lance called a *sarissa*, which was Philip's invention. It had a bladed head that was aimed at the face or the horse of an enemy trooper (who, with a shorter lance, couldn't reach the Macedonian cavalryman), and a spiked butt in case the rider missed on the first try. The Macedonians used a wedge formation for their cavalry, adopted from the Scythians, which gave them penetrating power and was easier to wheel about than the Greek square; and by the time Alexander launched his extraordinary campaign he had with him not only Macedonians, but also Thessalian and Thracian and some Persian cavalry totaling over 6,000. And this was just the beginning.

Philip had expanded and improved his Macedonian stock of horses, at one point importing, we are told, 20,000 mares; and we know from the Pazyryk burial sites in Siberia, which were roughly contemporary, that these would have been fine-limbed, and about fifteen hands. Many other excellent warhorses also came to strengthen the Macedonian cavalry of Alexander—from Thessaly, where Bucephalus was born, and from Thrace, which had a long history with horses, going back before the Greeks. To their own breeding stock— described by several commentators as easy keepers with impressive endurance, but ugly—the Thracians had added lines imported from Scythia. All of these stocks became part of Alexander's army.

His elite heavy horse guard was known as the Companion Cavalry, divided into units of around 200, with a special royal group numbering 300. To give a sense of the effectiveness of his cavalry, at the battle of the River Granicus in 334 BCE, Alexander's losses were about ninety horsemen—only twenty-five of them from the Companion Cavalry—along with thirty foot soldiers. Persian losses of cavalry and infantry were over 1,000.

The next year, at the battle of Issus, Alexander brought 4,500 cavalry against the Persian king Darius's 30,000. The Macedonians lost about 450 horse and foot soldiers; the Persians lost 15,000 men, and a lot of their horses were taken by Alexander after the battle.

Two years later, Alexander met Darius again near the Tigris River at Gaugamela. He now had 7,000 cavalry and 40,000 foot soldiers, while Darius had about 35,000 horse and a very large number of foot soldiers—estimates range from 200,000 to a million. He also had 200 four-horse scythe-wheel chariots—a type originally invented in India.

They didn't do him much good. The chariots themselves were easily dispatched by both foot soldiers and cavalry, since disabling any one horse immediately took out all four. And in the battles that followed, Macedonian losses were around 500—while the Persians lost close to 100,000 soldiers.

And Alexander was just getting warmed up. For the next eight years, he moved with his army across western Asia to India, gathering territory—and horses, to support his imperial adventures—along the way. The logistics were formidable, and were complicated beyond even his expectations by terrain that was, to say the least, unfriendly to horses (and not all that congenial to traveling humans). He shipped some supplies to local ports, offloading these onto baggage horses (each carrying up to 250 pounds), with the cavalry horses probably also packed.

We know surprisingly little about how these horses were packed up and their loads tied down, but both the rigging and the hitches used were almost certainly comparable to those that have come down through the centuries: the pack saddle, either sawbuck or Decker type, and a pair of panniers (also called kyacks or alforjas). The diamond hitch used in the mountains of the American West by packers to this day would probably have been recognized—or immediately adopted—by Alexander.

Then as now in difficult terrain, the horses usually carried their own food. Alexander paid very close attention to his horses' welfare—they were, after all, his most important military asset—and he allocated ten pounds of grain, ten pounds of hay, and up to eighty pounds of water a day for each horse, with (where possible) a day's rest each week for grazing. He also timed his forays to coincide with harvest dates in each region. These figures (reported from the time) are generous; but they give a sense of how carefully Alexander looked after his horses. Without them, he would have been—in every sense—nobody and nowhere.

He achieved some extraordinary feats on horseback. After Gaugamela, Alexander pursued Darius for a couple of days covering forty-six miles per day, and later, also chasing Darius, he and his troops rode about two hundred miles in five days through desert country on unshod horses, without water or enough food (only to find that Darius had been murdered by one of his commanders). In India, at the River Hydaspes, he even ran up against elephants in Porus's army, but he outmaneuvered them. When Alexander himself died less than two years later, in 323 BCE, he had established an empire that stretched from Greece to Afghanistan—and he had done it all with horses.

Although Alexander's victories signaled the effectiveness of swift, hard-hitting cavalry, it was Roman losses that confirmed it when they were routed by the Parthians (of Scythian origin) in 53 BCE, the Mauretanians in the third century CE, and by the Goths at the battle of Adrianopolis in 378 CE.

The Romans are rightfully credited with innovations that changed the world, creating the basis of our modern technological civilization with its efficient transportation and communication systems and its sophisticated legal regimes, industrial strategies, and military organizations. But when it came to horses, the Romans were followers rather than leaders. They learned quickly, and especially from their enemies. They mocked the Celtic and Germanic tribes as barbaric when they first saw them in combat; but then they learned through pain that this method of attack, involving a mix of cavalry and infantry, was remarkably effective. And they adopted arms and armor from the Persians, dividing the cavalry into *cataphractarii* (armored horsemen) and *clibarani* (where both rider and horse were armored). Together, these inspired the knights of the Middle Ages.

Then they did what all good imperialists do—they co-opted the locals. Before long, Goths and other Germanic cavalrymen were part of the Roman army, along with Huns and Mauretanians and Belmi from the Upper Nile, who are shown on the friezes of the Arch of Constantine in Rome. But for all their ingenuity, the Romans still relied heavily on their infantry, using the cavalry when they were most confident of victory. And they retained a visceral fear of the barbarians on horseback, so much so that in Rome all male citizens had to be dressed in togas and sandals rather than trousers and boots, since that was the attire of the wild hordes.

The Romans never turned their remarkable organizational talents to the specific training, careful selection of terrain, and constant attention to the welfare of the horses that cavalry demands—as Alexander had done so superbly. But horses were widely used in civil society, from the postal service to the chariot race. On a road system that stretched from Britain in the west to Syria in the east, horse-drawn mail coaches and freight carts—and express couriers on horseback—achieved a speed of transportation and communication that remained unmatched in Europe until the arrival of the train and the telegraph.

They introduced new breeds of horses—including hunters and draft horses, trotters and racers—throughout their empire. And they are usually credited with the invention of the horseshoe, in the first century CE, calling the metal soles they made with a piece that cupped over the top for attachment with leather thongs *hipposandals*—though Alexander might have already used boots on his horses' feet in rough terrain 350 years earlier.

In the Spanish peninsula, the Roman influence was strongly felt. Battling their great adversary Hannibal, the Romans invaded it late in the second century BCE, bringing horses of Eastern stock with them. Soon, they

A Roman mail coach (1st century BCE)

had established in the peninsula the races and other equestrian games that they were so fond of, and had begun to cross their horses with others from the region, resulting in the development of three main types: the ancestor of the Andalusian, close-coupled and round-bodied, substantial and swift; the elegant Jennet, with its fine gaits, rounded rump, and wavy mane; and the coarse and compact Gallic horse.

There are other influences that intersect with Roman horse culture. The success of Hannibal with horses, for example, lived on not only in his victories, but also in the Barb crosses with Etruscan horses that followed his time in Capua, near Naples, from 216 to 215 BCE. The result was the celebrated Neapolitan. While now extinct as a breed, two Neapolitan stallions were—with four other stallions of different breeds—founders of the Lippizaner line.

By the third century CE, camel riders from various nomadic tribes were part of the standing army of the Romans in North Africa, for at first the camel was the mount ridden by most warriors in the deserts there and in the Middle East. But the Arab peoples were already on the move into Egypt, Iraq, and Syria, and the Arab horse was to become the emblem of noble strength and beauty, bred for endurance as well as speed. Its exact provenance continues to be cloaked in those mists of time where the ancestors of today's horses hide, but one scholar of the breed, the nineteenth-century general Eugene Daumas, decided the matter as follows: "He lives between the sky and the sand. Call him Arabian, Barb, Turk, Persian, Nedji, it matters little, for all these terms are but baptismal names. The name of the family is Horse of the Orient."

There are a number of stories telling the origin of the Arab horse. Each of them sometimes varies a bit, as such stories do; but the message is always the same: the Arab horse comes from a very noble line.

> Muhammad's horses were thirsty, for he had kept them from water for a week to test their strength and loyalty. When he finally opened the gate and they all rushed out towards the watering hole, Muhammad sounded the call to battle. Five horses turned back. These five became his most trusted mounts, and their offspring the royal horses of Arabia.

In another account, Allah created the horse from the south wind, saying, "I want to make a creature out of you. Condense." And the wind did, whereupon the Archangel Gabriel took a handful of it to Allah, who made a horse the color of burnt chestnut, the color of the ant. And He hung happiness from the forelock between a horse's eyes.

And in yet another story the first horse breeder was Ishmael, Abraham's elder son and according to tradition the ancestor of the Arabs. That lineage continued with David, owner of over a thousand horses—so said Ibn al-Kalbi, who lived at the time of Muhammad and was famous for keeping the pedigree of Arab horses. When David died, his horses passed to his son Solomon, who chose one hundred from among them. Solomon eventually built up a stable of over 12,000 horses (thereby breaking Moses's decree, in Deuteronomy 17, that a king shall not multiply horses to himself); but from among that original one hundred a stallion known as Zad el-Raheb, or Gift to the Rider, was especially renowned. Solomon had presented him to certain Arabs who had come to Jerusalem from afar to pay tribute to the king on the occasion of his marriage to the Queen of Sheba. Grateful for their respect and recognizing the long and difficult journey back that they now faced, Solomon gave them the stallion to help them hunt along the way. Zad el-Raheb was faster than the zebra and the gazelle and the ostrich, and every hunt with him was successful, so when they arrived home they put him to stud—the legendary beginnings of the greatest line of purebred horses in the world.

There are rock paintings over 8,000 years old in what is now Libya that portray a horse remarkably like the modern Arab; and in a scientific account, the Arab horse is almost certainly descended from the Asiatic horses that came south to India thousands of years ago, while their northern kin went their own way.

The vision of horses having the kind of discipline and dedication that Muhammad sought—and thereby being an inspiration to humans—has been with us for a very long time. The loyal horse, like the noble horse, like the spirit horse, has no bounds of culture or country. It is the basis of the legendary Islamic love of horses, celebrated in the Qur'an and elaborated by Muhammad. It is the foundation of the great Christian tradition of chivalry, too, which shaped European civilization in the Middle Ages and influences it still. It is part of the sense, caught up in our celebration of wild horses, that spiritually as well as materially, psychologically as well as physically, we need horses. They run free, and become our friends, in our fields of dreams.

It was the noble horsemen of Arabia and the (then) newly founded religion of Islam that captured both the imagination of the world and territory across the Middle East, North Africa, and much of Spain in the centuries following the death of Muhammad in 632 CE. "By the snorting war steeds, which strike fire with their hoofs as they gallop to the raid at dawn and with a trail of dust cleave a massed army . . . ," begins Sura 100 of the Qur'an. The spread of Islam, like the spread of Christianity, depended on the conversion of the unfaithful; and from the beginning Muhammad recognized that military strength was the most efficient means to achieve this. The spiritual mission and the material care and control of horses became like warp and woof in the fabric of Islam.

This developed naturally from the situation that existed in the region before Muhammad. Horses provided transport for herding communities moving from place to place with their livestock. And tribal warfare, waged mostly on horseback, was routine. From Mecca, where he began, to Medina, where he fled in 622, Muhammad transformed both Arabia and the world. And while he did it ultimately with words, his deeds became legendary, both in war and peace. And he always gave credit to horses. During the decade in Medina until his death, he planned over sixty military campaigns, and personally led thirty of them; and his successor Abu Bakr drew on the discipline and dedication that Muhammad had inspired to extend power over much of the Middle East and North Africa, beginning with an attack on the Persians at Kadisiya.

Europe was a stubborn exception. In 711 CE, a force composed mostly of Muslim Berbers took the Rock of Gibraltar. During the next few years they moved across Spain and over the Pyrenees into France. But in 732, at Poitiers, the fast, light horses of the Moors ran up against the heavy—and heavily armed—lance horsemen of Charles Martel.

It was an archetypal conflict, not between good and evil as much as between guerrillas and gorillas. The gorillas won; but the guerrillas lived to fight another day. This was not the beginning of a new tradition of horse warfare —the Romans had used it, after all, and so did the Sarmatians with their lance warriors—but it seemed to mark a milestone in war as a testing ground for new equipment. In this case, larger and stronger horses, and heavier armor.

For nearly a millennium, the Spanish peninsula was the site of battles not only between Moors and Christians, but also between military technologies. The ancient Greek armor had consisted of a back and breast plate. The Romans used strips of metal, which allowed for much more freedom of movement. A further modification occurred with the introduction of linked chain mail, which was worn by Byzantine cavalrymen around 500 CE, and was still in use 500 years later when the Normans invaded England (as the Bayeux Tapestry confirms). Chain mail was heavy, so the horses needed to be as well. To meet the needs of the heavily armored lance horsemen, European cavalry supplemented the chain mail with plate armor to give additional protection to knees, arms, and shins, and before long knights were covered in complete suits of armor, with chain mail retained only for the neck and joints. Which meant even larger horses. And everyone got into the business of supplying them. Early in the twelfth century, monks of the Carthusian order began to breed horses, and they were among the first in Europe to maintain detailed records of each horse's pedigree.

But the Moors kept to their lighter mail armor and their purebred Barb stock, fast and agile and suited to the Asian and Middle Eastern cavalry style and its hit-and-run tactics. And elsewhere in Europe there were renewed demonstrations of its effectiveness, perhaps most impressively by the Hungarians, of Mongol descent, who began their raids into Europe in 883. Within a little more than a decade, they had reached Italy, bringing along packhorses to carry off plunder. Eventually, they ran up against the deadly enemy of nomadic peoples—scarce pasturage. This was the ultimate irony for a people who destroyed agricultural lands with an almost religious zeal. Still, like the Arabs, they swept across continents with a flair and a fury that is still recalled in story and song.

This worked until gunpowder, which probably originated in China as early as the ninth century CE, spread across Europe in the late Middle Ages. It came into intermittent use against cavalry in the middle of the fifteenth century, though it took a while before anyone figured out how best to use it on the field of battle. Hand-held guns—fairly awkward, and not very effective—were used by mounted soldiers in armies from the Spanish to the Swedish, mostly, it seems to scare everyone; and the ideology of the old days persisted long after firearms had become widely available, with cavalrymen in various cultures continuing to prefer close combat to the deadly but cowardly distance that crossbows and guns introduced. Swords were still the thing, insisted many—most spectacularly the Egyptian Mamelukes, a warrior caste of slaves originally from central Asia who were defeated by Ottoman guns in the early 1500s, and the Japanese samurai, who lived in a time and place where gunpowder was less widely available (for Japan had a system of gun control from the beginning of the seventeenth century that was very effective and culturally accepted). The horsemanship of both was remarkable, and their training closely resembled that of chivalric knights. Horsemen everywhere wanted to fight as their ancestors had. And for a long time, even after the revolver and the repeating rifle had come into use, they did just that.

There were brief returns to the days of bows and lances, and cavalry continued to play a part in war. In 1866 in the Austro-Prussian War, 56,000 cavalrymen armed with lance and saber went up against guns and rifles, and a few years later during the Franco-German War, 96,000 men rode into the field similarly armed in the last massed charge in military history. Mounted soldiers were still used during the First World War—the Russians had over 200,000 available—but badly deployed. It is tempting to say that cavalry made no difference in that war, but that wouldn't be true. A single division of German cavalry delayed the Russian army long enough to give Germany the victory at Tannenberg; and the British General Allenby used cavalry—supported by air power—effectively in Palestine against the Turkish army at the battle of Megiddo, one of the last battles with cavalry (and providing a befitting bookend to that earlier battle of Megiddo in 1469 BCE, the first fight with chariots of which we have a written record). By World War II, both the movement of troops and mobile attack were provided by the "new" mechanized and armored cavalry—tanks.

The horse was what war had been all about. Most of the stories and songs told of dashing horsemen and daring charges of heavy and light horse brigades, which were increasingly met with firepower or different tactics or unfriendly territory that often turned strength into weakness and life into death. For war, identified with chariotry and cavalry, was also inevitably associated with death. And for thousands of years this included the death of horses, catastrophic numbers of horses—like humans, dying not only from injury but from starvation, dehydration, and disease.

❦

Four hundred years after Poitiers—sometimes cited as the most important battle in the history of the West—the greatest nomadic horseman the world had ever seen rode out of the East. Born around 1162 CE, he began his adult life as a minor Mongolian warrior named Temujin; but he soon adopted the name Genghis Khan, meaning "ruler of all." And Temujin meant it. He conquered not just Mongolia and northern China (which he invaded after bringing together warring Mongol tribes) but much of Asia and parts of Europe. This was the triumph of the horsemen, living on horseback like centuries later the cowboys of the Americas, and covering whole continents.

The horsemen of Genghis Khan rode with what would later be called "natural equitation," controlling their horses more by knee action and shifts of weight than by the hands—giving the horses what Marco Polo described as freedom in their mouths—and allowing them to find their balance while the rider found his. The men were often in the saddle for days at a time, resting there while their horses grazed or feeding them from bundles of hay that they carried on their saddles; and on particularly tough treks they would feed themselves with blood drawn from their horses' veins.

Genghis Khan's achievement is best known from the account of Marco Polo, traveling two generations later across the Mongolian empire. The details of his battles are not available, mostly because there were not many people left to tell the tale, and his companions did not have either the ease or the inclination to do so; but what we have is evidence of maybe the greatest cavalry of all time, and a system of transportation and communication posts that

Mongol archer on horseback (China, Ming dynasty)

would make the architects of our contemporary "global network" envious: over 10,000 staging posts, at 25-mile intervals, each with a rest house and 400 horses drawn from local stock, half of them out to graze at any one time while the rest were available to be ridden by messengers.

⁂

Along with the incessant tribal conflicts in Europe and Asia during this period, two other major imperial enterprises emerged. One was the Christian Crusades and their counterpart, the Islamic response; and the other, a few centuries later, was the conquest of the Americas, first by Spanish and then by French and British invaders. Both were driven by a deadly mix of material and spiritual ambition, and both were undertaken with horses. Boats got them across the Mediterranean and the Atlantic, and then along the lakes and riverways; but horses were the primary instrument of these horrific "holy wars."

Perversely, love is frequently at the still center of the turning world of war. Love of country, of riches, of land, of adventure, of a god, of another woman or man—this, along with jealousy, is what war is so often about. Horses have been at the heart of this contradiction from the beginning, which may be one of the reasons they are so often associated with the spiritual. *Ecstasies of Love and War*, reads the subtitle of a book by Dudley Young called *Origins of the Sacred*.

Nowhere is this contradiction more obvious than in the concept of chivalry. In one of those bittersweet historical ironies, the chivalric tradition that eventually became associated with the Christian Crusades was almost certainly influenced by Islamic courtly traditions, as well as by Germanic military initiations and of course Christian ideals of devotion and sacrifice. In historical terms, chivalry may have roots elsewhere too, for in China a thousand years earlier there was a tradition of the wandering romantic, on horseback in service to others.

But mostly, the European tradition mirrored that of the Arabs, with the horse at its core; and in some ways, both were the products of similar cultures, with all the paraphernalia of the time: slaves, serfs, and masters; small communities with strong tribal affiliations; local militia organized around local allegiances. On the whole, the Arabs treated their horses better than the Europeans did, and they may have been better horsemen; but that aside, these two social and economic—and religious—institutions were unmatched for bringing together horses and humans in a pact of honor and duty, and in the service of both love and war.

Chivalry in Europe carried a cluster of other contradictions. Gentleness and force. The spiritual and the secular. Art and life. Lancelot and Joan of Arc. Horses are the archetypal in-betweeners, and chivalry was the archetypal horse culture.

It all came down, as it so often does with both humans and horses, to a set of conventions. Conventions are the core constitutions of societies, and the basis of all systems of equitation. Humans and horses live by rituals and routines; and in the uncertain world of European feudalism, with local jurisdictions having a hodgepodge of different conventions, chivalry provided both.

Muhammad gave the tribes that he brought together under the shield of Islam a holy empire based upon a semi-nomadic horse culture. Chivalry gave Europe an ideal of wandering within the reality of a settled society, the chivalric knight having one eye on the horizon and the other on his home (preferably a castle). Like the nomadic warrior of the steppes, the medieval knight was a lonesome dove, a carefree cowboy with a strict set of rules, a traveler who would never settle down but dreamed about doing so. The chivalric code demanded a warrior spirit and a compassionate sensibility, civilized in principle and barbaric in practice. And its hallmark was meditation in action, which not surprisingly was also the basis of good horsemanship. Like the horse that was its body and soul, chivalry hovered between freedom and discipline, and between the real and the imagined.

In Wolfram von Eschenbach's *Parzival*, the early thirteenth-century tale of a knight's quest for the Holy Grail, we learn of Parzival's great distress when he sees three drops of blood on a blanket of snow in the forest. They remind him of his lost love, and he is in a deep trance, staring down from his horse onto the snow, when one of King Arthur's knights challenges him. The next few moments provide an image of chivalry, suspended between love and war, virtue and violence, dreaming and waking . . . and absolutely dependent upon a horse.

> As he gazed at the drops of blood Parzival was so over-
> whelmed by the memory of love that he did not even
> notice the knight, who had wheeled around to attack
> him with his lance. But Parzival's horse turned towards

the enemy and away from the blood in the snow, bringing Parzival back to his senses and to the danger now facing him. He fixed his own lance and braced himself to take a blow on his shield. He did so; but his lance was so well aimed that the other knight was knocked off his horse. Not even pausing to ask his assailant's name, Parzival rode back to the drops of blood and was once again lost to the pains of love.

Intensity and nonchalance, both of them exaggerated, and both bound together in one poetic moment.

A medieval tournament (Switzerland, 13th century)

Everything was exaggerated in the chivalric mode, including the size of the horses. "Great horses," as they were called, were bred specially in what became a kind of medieval arms race; and true to form much else became exaggerated too, including clothing and equipment. Medieval riding techniques were different from both nomadic and modern ones, with saddles that were like the seat of a racing car, leaving little room for movement, with much of the pressure taken on legs that would have been nearly straight and securely set in stirrups. The bits and bridles were massive and mean-looking, though the knights must have used them with a relatively light touch —much lighter than many would advocate today—or they would have ruined every horse they sat. Actually, they probably brought very little pressure at all to bear on the horse's mouth, settled as deep as they were in their saddles and surrounded by armor.

Tournaments were the cherished event where all this was played out, literally and figuratively. They were originally a training ground for war, and then they turned into its imitation. In the turmoil of everyday feudal conflicts, the tournament must have offered a relative haven of order and discipline, transcending the chaos of local practices. In sports terms, they were more like the "settled" sports of American football or cricket than "nomadic" sports like soccer or hockey. Rules for jousting tournaments were set down by a Frenchman named Geoffroi de Purelli in 1066, the same year that the Normans rode all over the English at Hastings; unfortunately, de Purelli himself was killed on his first outing. A tournament *was* risky, like the field of battle that was its model. But by the time they came into wide currency as popular entertainment, the battlefield had changed; and long before Don Quixote rode across the Mancha, the knight in shining armor had become tactically obsolete. But he still cut a fine figure, at least in the medieval imagination.

The new times were hard on chivalry, and positively humiliating for the poorer knights who had few other sources of support than what came to them from war and robbery. So the best of them became professional players in a dangerous game, their skills stylized beyond recognition, just as they are in the professional rodeo of today.

⤚

Eventually, art and life made up with each other again, and humans and horses started another dance. Beginning around the fifteenth century—and for the first time since antiquity—Europeans began to theorize about practical things and to put theory into practice when it came to horses and riding, just like their explorers and conquistadors were doing with regard to boats and navigation as they began to circle the world. The society that developed in the Renaissance not only gave pride of place to horses, as the arts and crafts of the time demonstrate; it combined this with a fascination for travel. It was wandering and settling once again, with horses and humans as co-conspirators.

With the rediscovery of a variety of classical texts during the Renaissance—including the training manuals of Xenophon, advocating the humane treatment of horses, and the writings of the thirteenth-century equestrian expert Abu Bekr-ibn-Bedr, from the court of the Sultan of Cairo—there emerged a new interest in equitation as an art form. Schools of equitation developed theories in which principles of courtly behavior rested comfortably beside those on the care and training of horses, just as they had in seventh- and eighth-century Islam and would again in eighteenth- and nineteenth-century native American culture. Alongside, a remarkable equestrian literature came into its own, and conversations about horses, along with poems and paintings and professional opinions about them, surpassed other kinds of learning and became almost as important as the horses themselves. In a way, horses provided the rhetorical signature of a rhetorical age.

Horses became a preoccupation of rich families, just as luxury and racecars are today. Baldassarre Castiglione—one of the exemplars of the Renaissance and the author of its classic, *The Courtier*—bred horses for his noble relative Federico Gonzaga and supervised their success at the racetrack. He even contributed to the founding of the classic English racing stock by encouraging Gonzaga to present Henry VIII with a few of his celebrated mares in 1533. Henry then added some mares from the great Turin stud farm, and so brought Oriental blood into the lineage of English racehorses.

Just as Italian culture was the heart and soul of the Renaissance, so Italian horses were for a time the pride of Europe. Hardly surprising, then, it was an Italian, Don Prospero d'Osma, who was called in by Elizabeth I to bring some order to the English breeding program. His report, written in 1576, praised the outstanding Italian mares held at the royal stud, but advocated careful attention to maintaining pure bloodlines and avoiding the mixing of breeds. Miscegeny, once again, was out. But Arab horses were definitely in.

During the Middle Ages, the adventures of chivalry and the Crusades had kept the horse busy in wars and tournaments, as well as pulling carts and plowing fields. Although artists portrayed all of these subjects, religious themes were overwhelmingly favored, and—except for statues and sculptures like Charlemagne on horseback or the Rider in the cathedral in Bamberg—the horse all but disappeared as an emblem of worldly authority. Of course, death sometimes rode on horseback, which helped keep the horse in the picture, morbidly situated in between the secular and the sacred.

But the artists of the Renaissance brought the horse back with fanfare, from Paolo Uccello and Piero della Francesca, Andrea Mantegna and Sandro Botticelli, to Albrecht Dürer and Pieter Brueghel the Elder. Now there were both formal explorations (such as Leonardo da Vinci's horse studies for monuments in Milan, and Michelangelo's drawings) and themes ranging from classical mythology (often including portraits of a noble patron's horses) and war (celebrating both the battles themselves and the victorious leaders) to that exemplar of

Renaissance culture, the hunt, where the barbaric and the civilized met. Motifs such as St. George and the Dragon brought together the hunt and the battle, the local and the legendary, and provided a link between the late Middle Ages and the Renaissance. In religious art, too, horses now played an important part in paintings and frescoes, from the Adoration of the Magi to the Crucifixion. In many ways the horse was one of the central subjects of Renaissance art.

By the seventeenth century, artists began to pick up the poses of *haute école*; soon statues with riders performing elegant moves on horseback began to appear on every square in town. And with the breeding success of the English Thoroughbred and the increasing popularity of racing as a social as well as an economic phenomenon, the horse race became a major subject of the arts. War scenes, with cavalry and foot soldiers on a bloody battlefield, were now hung alongside horses and spectators on a picturesque racecourse.

≈

When Columbus made his second voyage to the "new" world of the Americas in 1494, he brought twenty-four stallions and ten mares with him, along with a significant

The Battle of San Romano in 1432 (Paolo Uccello, ca. 1455)

number of cattle. On the island of Hispaniola where he landed, the animals thrived, creating in remarkably short order a surplus of wild, ownerless cattle, along with skilled horsemen who adapted Spanish equestrian techniques and equipment to the new environment. When settlement spread to the mainland, horses and cattle migrated across the continent, and by the late seventeenth century, the foundations for the cowboy cultures of the Western Hemisphere had been laid. And for the great horse cultures of native America.

Other equestrian instincts also came into play. The historian Bernal Diaz del Castillo, serving under Cortez, recorded the name, pedigree, color, sex, and qualities of every single one of the horses who came to Mexico in 1519. It was a tribute to the importance of the horse in the Americas. And a signal that she was back.

Some horses didn't make it across the ocean. One of the most poignant testimonials to their fate survives in the term *horse latitudes*, which refers to the zone 30° to 35° north and 30° to 35° south of the equator near the tropics of Cancer and Capricorn, where ships would often become becalmed. Sometimes, in desperation, the sailors would throw horses overboard to preserve water and lighten their load.

But many horses did make it; and although the conquistadors' horses were slow to adapt to the tropical regions of the Caribbean, Central America, Venezuela, and Brazil, when they got to the pampas of Argentina and the plains of the American Southwest, they knew that they were home. One Pedro de Mendoza fed five mares and seven stallions amidst the starving colonists in his charge, and then set them free to roam. Within a few years, the pampas were, in the words of Vazquez de Espinosa (writing at the beginning of the seventeenth century), "covered with escaped horses in such numbers that when they go anywhere they look like woods from a distance." Around the same time, horses were spreading out over the North American plains, and one traveler reported in 1777 that in the Rio Grande area of Texas there were so many horses that "their trails make the country, utterly uninhabited by people, look as if it were the most populated in the world."

The indigenous people took to horses in different ways. Initially, the Spanish were careful not to let horses into enemy hands; but the Pueblo Revolt of 1680 resulted in large numbers of horses escaping. Even so, in Mexico the Indians responded cautiously. By contrast, within a generation of acquiring their first horses (mostly by theft), the Apaches and Comanches were doing things on horseback that astonished even the Spaniards, who were excellent horsemen. But the ironies were also grim, as the horse became an instrument of destruction, used by the invaders to overwhelm the indigenous peoples. This was the old story, going back thousands of years. "After God, we owe our victory to our horses," said the Spanish conquistadors, echoing the nomadic warriors on the steppes, whose language was different but who also gave thanks for their horses.

But the horse became an instrument of defense as well; in response to the Spanish invaders, the plains Indians made it part of their warfare, praising horses as a gift of *their* Creator as their dynamic Indian cultures flourished in another kind of Renaissance, which produced art as exquisite as any, and equestrian craft that was second to none.

≋

The European Renaissance, for its part, sponsored a new aesthetic sensibility even as it sponsored the invasion of indigenous lands around the world. The barbaric was paired with the civilized, as style and savagery danced together. In the centers of civility, in elegant arenas with fashionable audiences, riders performed movements that imitated those of war, just as they had in the sports and riding competitions that had taken place on the Eastern steppes so long ago. It was in those Renaissance halls of Europe, within the strict disciplines of the riding school, that the parade moves of the archetypal victory were displayed—the *passage* and the *piaffe*, and then the *volte*, the *levade*, the *pesade*, the *pirouette*, and the *capriole*, all moves of the battlefield. Or of the workplace; the pirouette, for instance, was a fancy name for something that every herder on a horse would do every time an animal needed to be cut off or cut out.

But this was Renaissance Europe, and like everywhere else it wanted to have its own way with horses. The codification of a new horse culture was under way, one that transcended the dichotomies of war and peace, as well as of work and play. Accordingly, the so-called classical riding school took shape, a rediscovery of Egyptian and Greek artifice along with Arab and Eastern flair. Sixteenth-century treatises like those by Federico Grisone and Giovanni Pignatelli provided an equestrian counterpart to the courtly manifestos of Castiglione and Machiavelli, rich in the prescription of virtue and style. They were followed in the seventeenth century by Solomon de la Broue, Antoine de Pluvinel, Gaspart de Saunier, and William Cavendish (the Duke of Newcastle). It was François Robichon de la Guérinière, writing in the eighteenth century, who made the greatest contribution, not only insisting on much more flexible training methods but also the development of "an air of ease and freedom" that he described with the simple word "grace." His methods were the foundation for the great Spanish Riding School in Vienna, which, together with the Cavalry School at Saumur in France, now provides the only training that meets the high school standards of haute école, the virtuoso performance of "airs above ground."

Classical dressage, for all its elaborate trappings, simply stylized some basic equestrian techniques, from riding in a circle to wheeling and turning in more or less intricate ways. These fundamentals had both functional and formal appeal: they played a part in cavalry maneuvers and cattle roundups, and they could be both elegant and entertaining. Haute école provided ceremonial display to a society that admired discipline and decorum on the one hand, and extravagance and excess on the other.

These contradictions led naturally into the circus, which brought the horse back to the people in performances that took the moves of the dressage arena and transformed them in a show ring under a (nomadic) tent. The circus was, in every sense, theater in the round. Of course, acrobatic tricks on horseback had been performed for millennia, maybe beginning with the day on which that first girl to ride out there on the steppes would have called out all excited, "Look, ma, no hands!"; and young riders would have been anxious throughout the ages to show off to each other. Acrobatics have also been part of military training from the Roman to the Russian cavalry, and of entertainments like the games of ancient Greece.

The genius of the circus was in the ring itself—which

is what *circus* meant in Latin. The person usually credited with inventing the modern circus—one Philip Astley, a sometime sergeant major in the British cavalry—discovered that he could keep his balance while standing on a horse if it ran around in a circle. In 1769, he built the first circular track of its kind, and within fifteen years one of his riders had established the Royal Circus in London. Astley's ring has kept not only that name but its size, about forty feet in diameter, and the combination of the smooth gait of a slow canter or a full gallop and the centrifugal force on the rider as the horse leaned into the center made it possible to perform extraordinary feats, apparently defying both

A circus poster

gravity and good sense—which was exactly what the spectators were there to see. The horses ranged from hot-blooded, high-stepping Hackneys to cool-running, easygoing Percherons, with gray or white Arabs—and occasionally, a legendary Lippizaner—taking the fanciest parts. Haute école made the artificial seem natural. The circus did the opposite.

By the end of the nineteenth century, the circus had become an icon of modernist culture, the place where art and life came together, along with princes and paupers, in appropriately paradoxical juxtaposition: the upper classes sat on the lower level, in the boxes along the sawdust-covered floor, while the lower classes were high up in the grandstand. Painters like Toulouse-Lautrec and Degas and later Picasso made the circus one of their favorite subjects; but eventually the music hall took over the trade from the circus, and horses returned to the battlefields one last time in World War I.

❧

One of the greatest horse paintings of all time was done in England during the eighteenth century, by George Stubbs. He had started out as a society portrait painter, but he became fascinated with animals—and especially horses—to such an extent that he dedicated almost ten years of his life to a detailed study of "the anatomy of a horse," which he published (in 1766) under that title.

But Stubbs also painted racehorses and hunting scenes, and in 1762 he was commissioned by the Marquis of Rockingham to paint a stallion named Whistlejacket. It was originally planned that Stubbs's painting of the horse would be complemented by a portrait of King George III (to be painted by another artist), on an appropriate picturesque

Whistlejacket (George Stubbs, 1762)

background (by yet a different artist), all on the same canvas. But for whatever reasons—the shifting political landscape may have been the most important—Whistlejacket stands alone. In every sense.

The painting shows the horse rearing from a levade, down on his hocks (or haunches) and gathering himself to rear up or lunge ahead at the enemy. Done against an unpainted background that highlights the splendid conformation and spirit of the horse, it is a stunning piece of art. It represents an image straight from the riding academies of the Renaissance, in which this was one of the moves a horse would have displayed to demonstrate the ultimate in civilized control. It was a very popular pose, picked up by artists from Rubens and Velasquez to Goya and David, in their portraits of men of war from Alexander to Napoleon.

But Stubbs's painting also represents an image of raw power and wildness. Whistlejacket, in fact, was an almost unmanageable horse. He apparently caught a glimpse of the completed painting when Stubbs leaned it against a wall, and turned to attack it with such determination that he lifted his groom (who was holding him by the bridle) right off the ground. And although his untamed nature is not itself the subject of the painting, Stubbs catches something that was part of the tradition of equitation: the violence of battle.

It was one of the precepts of haute école that the moves in which horses were schooled were derived from war. So the levade, it was argued, gave the rider an opportunity to use his spear against a cowering enemy, while the horse struck him with his hooves. The most advanced of the airs above ground which are the highlight of this tradition of riding is the capriole, where the horse jumps straight up in the air from a standstill to a height of about six feet, kicks out its hind legs, and then lands right back where it started. Apparently this would give horse and rider in battle an opportunity to escape when they were surrounded.

Many have claimed that these were practical moves, and cleared the way for victory. Surely they were advertised that way; and Xenophon even describes something similar in his writings. But that must have been mostly theory. The levade and the capriole take quiet and concentration, almost meditative calm, which is usually in short supply on the battlefield.

War stories often work this way, but war itself is different. If horse and rider were to try this in battle, the scene would probably play out like the one in *Raiders of the Lost Ark*, where Indiana Jones (Harrison Ford) is confronted by a menacing man who goes through an astonishing set of martial-arts moves, fearsome and fast. After standing there for a moment, Indiana Jones pulls out his gun and shoots the fellow. Any horse that launched itself into a levade or a capriole in the midst of a battle would most likely have met the same fate—some soldier on the ground would have shot it. The killing of horses, after all, goes back to the very beginnings of human history.

Chapter 5

GREAT HORSE
CULTURES
OF THE WORLD

From Ancient China to Modern Europe

All discussions of the civilized and the barbaric are ultimately about culture: what is it, who has it, how does it determine differences in land use and language and livelihood? For thousands of years, horses have shaped these differences and defined the cultures of many peoples. They have also provided common ground between them.

The irony about the great civilizations that were

shaped by horses is that most of them—like the Mongolians and the Scythians and the Huns and the Apaches and the Comanches and the Blackfoot—were usually dismissed as uncivilized, with no culture at all.

As we have seen, the conflict between barbaric and civilized peoples is as old as humanity. It's the age-old clash between Them and Us, and in the early days it took the form of a confrontation between settled folk, dedicated to a particular place and to managing the uncertainties of life, and wandering peoples who seemed to welcome uncertainty, living nowhere in particular with attachments to nothing permanent and ever ready to strike anywhere and destroy everything. Terrorizers.

There were none more frightening to settled societies than nomadic horsemen. And there were no nomadic horsemen more frightening than the nomads of the steppes. They fought to win; they fought for the spoils; and they fought for the sake of fighting. Their fighting wasn't for sovereignty, and it wasn't for survival. It was, in its way, spiritual.

The art of war for the Mongols and their kin was an art for art's sake, highly sophisticated and deeply cultured. Of course it had its material side. The nomads converted the horse-drawn wagon into the shopping cart of the steppes, using it to carry off booty; and since they measured prestige and power by the quantity and quality of their horses, any horses in an enemy camp would immediately be added to their stock. But at the end of the day, asking why they went on raids would be like asking why Crop Eared Wolf stole horses.

The nomads presented a challenge for much longer than is usually acknowledged, and much further west. For nearly a century, medieval Europe itself was under siege by them in the form of the Normans in the north, the Muslims in the south, and the Magyars in the east. The Magyars—or Hungarians—were an Asian tribe who had first raided into Europe in the late ninth and early tenth centuries, riding as far west as Italy, Burgundy, and Germany. They were eventually defeated in 955 by a German army under Emperor Otto I, and they quickly converted to Christianity (a strategic move to avoid being absorbed into the Byzantine empire); but they were a reminder of the globalization of equestrian traditions that had been going on for thousands of years. People in the ancient, medieval, and early modern world grumbled about the Mongolization of their culture the way many people grumble today about Americanization; and although the world has changed, the hold of the horse hasn't, and Mongolia still leads the way. It is the only part of our planet where horses (three million of them) outnumber humans.

Yet we need to be careful about identifying the first horse culture, however tempting it is to claim that honor for the nomads of the Asian steppes, or for some anonymous community on the banks of the Oxus, the river that separates central Asia from Persia and the Middle East, and from which, some say, horses and riders first went out to war. In important ways, the culture of horses begins with the peoples who painted horses on the walls of caves twenty and thirty and maybe forty or fifty thousand years ago, peoples for whom horses were more than meat, more than a means to get here and there, more than a way of waging war or wagering who'll win a race. Horses, for them, were something to praise and paint and carve and collect. Horse culture begins there.

Something else began there, as it did with hunting and gathering societies around the world, many of whom did not have horses: a way of working with the world, of negotiating with its natural and supernatural powers.

Horses made this easier in the communities of central Asia where finding a way meant moving around. The cave paintings suggest that horses helped humans long before they were domesticated, and that they were respected and revered long before they were roped and ridden.

We know little about these nomadic civilizations, though what we do know defies all the stereotypes about the civilized and the barbaric. They struggled to survive and had little time for sentimentality; but they celebrated their sovereignty and made time for ceremonies. They had a complex set of social and spiritual affiliations that would rival those of settled societies, and an understanding of how the same horses that helped them establish a balance with the world could also help them upset that balance.

The Chinese, who watched the nomads first over the horizon and then over the Great Wall—which they built to keep the northern invaders out—took to horses in the same inventive and imaginative way they took to so much else, making chariots and harnesses and carvings and paintings that count among the finest in the history of horses and humans. They drove horses, and they rode them; they raced horses, and they raided other people's herds; they developed ways of training and treating horses that were both specific to their circumstances and became of universal interest.

Horses had first been domesticated in China very early, probably about five thousand years ago, but it wasn't until around 1500 BCE that they became important for transport in general and for war in particular, where one battle cart could carry fifty foot soldiers. Their horses were small, stocky, and strong; but confronted with the smash-and-grab cavalry of the Hsiung-nu, or Huns—from whom they adopted both tack (saddle and stirrup) and battle tactics—and the failure of the Great Wall to provide adequate defense, the Chinese began breeding horses for more size and speed, and arming their cavalry with lance and sword and bow. The importance of this has survived in the terracotta figures—including horses measuring seventeen hands—entombed in the extraordinary mausoleum that was completed soon after Emperor Qin Shi Huang's death in 210 BCE.

When warring factions had been brought into line and China's power was consolidated during the Han dynasty, which began in 202 BCE, horses took their place in a Confucian ideology that was somewhere between medieval chivalry and Renaissance refinement, with a

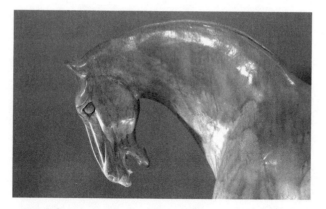

Tomb figure of a Ferghana horse (China, T'ang dynasty)

gentry trained in the literary classics and (to a lesser extent) equestrian skills. The Hsiung-nu, however, formed their own confederacy and remained a formidable threat until Wu-ti, the so-called Martial Emperor, came to power in 140 BCE. It was Wu-ti who brought Chinese culture and the horse into Korea and Japan, and who sent his expeditionary forces to the west to get the heavenly horses of Ferghana; and the elegance of these horses—with their fine heads, long curved necks, and muscular hindquarters—became the model for the depiction of horses in bronze and wood and clay, culminating in the marvelous pottery figures of the T'ang dynasty (which lasted from 618 to 907 CE).

One of the indications of the sophistication of a culture is the distinction its language makes between things. N|u, the language of the ≠Khomani Bushmen of southern Africa, has different names for plants and animals at different times and in different phases of their life. Inuktitut, the language of Inuit (Eskimo) peoples, has a wide range of words to distinguish different types of snow, while Peruvians have many words for varieties and conditions of the potato, a staple of their diet.

Most horse cultures are rich in names for everything to do with horses—from their colors, their personalities, and the parts of their bodies to their natural habits, learned movements, and uses. The Chinese have an exceptionally large number of words in their languages for talking about horses; the same is true for languages as different as Kazak and Kainai and Icelandic. Arabic even uses different forms of a word for the same color of stallions and mares; *az-rak* and *zar-ka* refer to a light blue-gray, and *ab-rash* and *bar-sha* describe a flea-bitten gray (with black or bay pencil-marks coming out of a white or gray coat).

Such words constitute a jargon, a language both specific and strange. These jargons differ in detail from culture to culture, but they create common ground between those who share the technical knowledge. In this sense, horses sponsored one of the first craft guilds, and the craftsmen of the horse were those who were expert not only in training but also in talking about them.

This kind of technical vocabulary has informed the languages of all horse cultures, from Asia and northern Africa to Europe and the Americas. For instance, a random selection from a long catalogue of the words that the English language still uses to identify the illnesses and ailments of horses will be clear and precise to the initiate, but mystifying to outsiders: sweeney, splints, stringhalt, thoroughpin, thrush, farcy, glanders, bog spavin, dummy, hoofer, stifles, curb, capped hock, wind gall, wind puff, thick wind and broken wind, sidebone, poll-evil, thrush, founder, quittor, and seedy toe. Some words have fallen out of use, like these two that were still used back in the 1880s: mallenders (described in an all-purpose "Stock Doctor" book of the time as "scurfy manifestations at flexions of the knees, sometimes becoming cracked and itchy") and sallenders (the same around the hock).

Anyone who spends any time around horses will be introduced to this horse-talk, and to the semi-secret society which controls it and of which we are either insiders or outsiders . . . like the otherwise immensely knowledgeable Samuel Johnson, who in his famous dictionary—the first in the English language—defined "pastern" as the knee of a horse. Asked by a lady more learned about such matters than he was why he made such a stupid mistake—the pastern is more like a horse's ankle, though that's not quite right, either—Johnson candidly replied, "Ignorance, ma'am. Pure ignorance."

Knowledge of horses is a great equalizer. It can be a great unifier, too, for it exists across classes and cultures that often have little else in common with each other, and it brings people together—in their imaginations, at least, where we all live much of the time anyway—from dry deserts and fertile valleys, open plains and hunched up hills, people who might be hunters or herders, cowboys or Indians, farmers or city folk.

From Asia to the Americas, and from the country racecourse to the city circus, horses became an indispensable part of the livelihoods, the languages, and the leisure time of many peoples, valued not only for the various practical possibilities that they embodied but also for their embodiment of something—a bond, a balance, a beauty—beyond the everyday.

This ideal reached a peak in ancient times with a people who, in comparison with many of their contemporaries, didn't *use* horses much at all: the Greeks. Maybe the extraordinary legacy of their civilization to Western culture begins with their capacity to take something useful like a horse and make it useless in the way art is useless; in the way ten or a hundred or a thousand horses—rather than two or three—are useless to a Kazak or a Navajo family; in the way life-size terra-cotta horses or exquisite clay figurines are useless to the dead emperors who keep them company in those ancient tombs in China.

In some ways the roots of modernity in Europe lie not in the remarkable contributions of the ancient Greeks to democracy and rhetoric in politics, individuality and responsibility in social life, public and private enterprise in economics, and apparently endless arguments between religion and science, but in the transformation of the horse from a beast of burden and a weapon of war into a figure of restless or rebellious beauty and an icon of spiritual grace.

And yet of course this transformation wasn't modern at all. It was as ancient as humanity, a return to the graceful curving figures of those cave paintings, and to the gymnastic skills and the games and the gambling and the stories and songs in which horses have played a central part for so long, and which found favor with the Greeks in the West and the Chinese in the East and in the cult of the horse in the Muslim and Christian cultures that came later.

The Greek fascination with the horse defied all sorts of logic, which was undoubtedly part of its appeal. Greece is mainly a mountainous country, more heavily wooded in antiquity than now, and quite unlike the open land to the east where the horse was at home. But the Greeks made the horse *feel* at home on their peninsulas and islands. That was an act of domesticating genius that we have been trying to repeat ever since.

Horses were probably first brought to the region by the Thessalians, who in turn got them from Cimmerian and Scythian steppe horsemen as well as from the Medes and the Persians. In Persia horses had been known from early times, and played an important part in society. The Persian name for a horse, *aspa*—after the Sanskrit *asva*—figures in the names of many places and people in the region.

But the Greeks took to the horse in a special way. They portrayed horses exquisitely on vases and friezes, in sculptures and drinking cups. They carved horses on great buildings like the Parthenon, and their images still enthrall us; and they spoke about horses in detail and delight, from Homer to Xenophon. They raced horses with an attention to tactics and breeding much as we do, and they celebrated the winners just like us.

Their gods were well acquainted with horses, specializing in chariots and the ancient equivalent of car chases. In a Mediterranean version of the Blackfoot myth of the origin of the horse from the old mallard, a Cretan legend has the horse rising out of the sea when the trident of Poseidon struck the rock of the Peloponnesus. Horses figure in the fables of earth, air, and fire as well as water, transporting the gods even to the underworld when Hades carries Persephone off in a chariot drawn by black horses. The winged Pegasus carts around thunder and lightning for Zeus; one of the twelve labors of Hercules is to capture the man-eating horses of King Diomedes of Thrace (which Hercules achieves by killing the king and feeding him to his horses, thereby taming them); and Ares, son of Zeus and god of war, rides in a chariot driven by his cheerful sons Deimos (Fear) and Phobos (Terror). On the Parthenon frieze, an exhausted horse driven by Selene the goddess of the moon is depicted opposite the fresh horses of the sun god Helios.

Like the gods themselves, horses were admired by the Greeks for their volatility and unpredictability, their seemingly insatiable need for attention to be paid and respect to be shown, their love of physical as well as metaphysical grooming. Horses and the art that they inspired became studies in the contradictions of the ideal life: rebellious

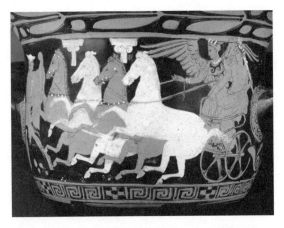

Hercules Ascending to Olympus in a Chariot
(Greece, ca. 400 BCE)

repose; self-importance slipping into submission; the certainty of surprise. With horses, as with gods, it was never over until it was over.

The Greeks raced their horses on all sorts of occasions, both sacred and secular. Early in the history of the Olympic Games (in 680 BCE) chariot races were introduced, with mounted (bareback) horse races added thirty-two years later and saddle horse races beginning in 564 BCE. These were long races, nearly fifteen miles (twelve times around a mile-and-a-quarter track), and they attracted many of the famous—and infamous—figures of the time. At the 47th Olympics, the wealthy Alcmaeon won with horses loaned to him by the even wealthier Croesus. The Athenian tyrant Pisistratus won at the 62nd Olympics, in a year in which Pythagoras experimented with a diet of meat instead of dried figs for the athletes. And Alcibiades the Athenian brought sponsorship to a modern level when he entered seven *quadrigas* at the games in 416 BCE, taking first, second, and fourth place. Alexander the Great allegedly said he would participate only if all the other contestants were kings, though his father, Philip, not so snobbish, had competed in the games in 356 BCE. The story goes that Philip was more delighted with his win at the Olympics than with the news—which came the same day—of the birth of his son Alexander and a crucial military victory at Potidaea. He had a coin minted showing him driving his victorious chariot.

As the games changed from religious festivals to sporting events, the congregations changed too, and by Roman times racing had all the trappings of modern sports, with large crowds, big money, fierce partisanship, doping scandals, and betting (both on-track and off-track, with results taken to the bookmakers by carrier pigeon). Horse racing continued to be popular under the Byzantine emperors, flourishing for a thousand years in Constantinople.

By the time of the Crusades, the contradictions associated with the horse in Greek art had been transferred to the knight, this infinitely ambiguous medieval figure, and the horse became symbolic of all the contradictions at the heart of the chivalric tradition. Although the Crusaders came from a European society in which ignorance and superstition had a firm seat, at least some of them realized that the Islamic world of that time was in many respects a place of remarkable light and learning, as well as remarkable horsemanship. In 1066, the year the Normans defeated the English and the first chivalric jousting tournament was held, Baghdad had over thirty colleges, some of them attended by women; Muslim Spain had over seventy public libraries; and Omar Khayyam was writing poetry that would still be read a thousand years later. Horses and learning went hand in hand.

꩜

No horse culture quite matched that of the Arabs for its discipline and its devotion. From the time of Muhammad, horses were included within a wide range of codes and customs that flowed from the Prophet, or were inscribed in the Qur'an. Like other societies both ancient and modern, Arabs saw the horse as a gift, one which vested on humans a responsibility not only of gratitude but of respect, and which provided both a source of spiritual and material rewards and a way of earning a living and not being a burden to others.

The conservatism of Arab society, in which everything had its enduring place, ensured that the horse remained an important part of the culture, to whom blessings were connected till the Day of Judgment; and the care of a horse was identified as a form of noble charity (one of the five pillars of Islam). The training of horses, too, was as

Muhammad (shown faceless according to Islamic tradition), the First Three Caliphs, and an Archangel (early 17th century)

disciplined as the Islamic rituals. The horse was brought home into Arab tents; but on the other hand, a Muslim would never give a horse a person's name. Rather, the most noble animals were given names that reflected their disposition, their color, or their abilities, a tradition continued in the naming of celebrated racehorses around the world. The respect accorded to horses in Arab society also took other forms, some of which set ideals against realities, just as medieval chivalry did. For example, Islamic law forbade the gelding of horses; but the luxury of obeying that law was usually available only to rich families, since the poor could seldom afford the time and trouble to look after more than one stallion.

Like Islam itself, Arab horse culture was first of all a culture of the desert, where grain was sometimes even scarcer than water. This made many equestrian practices close to those of the steppes and plains, semi-arid environments where feeding routines differed significantly from those in agricultural Europe. Among the Arabs, crushed dates were often substituted for grain, and ewe's or camel's milk along with local grasses, aromatic herbs, and the roots and leaves of some bushes were fed to horses. Traditionally, they were kept lean, watered only once around midday. "Water at dawn makes a horse thin, water at dusk makes him fat" is an old Arab saying. If grain was fed, it was also at midday: "The morning barley will be found on the dung heap [having passed right through the horse], the evening barley on the rump [as fat]."

The Qur'an refers to horses as El-Kheir, the supreme blessing, and Muhammad spoke often about horses, with his words and deeds preserved in the *hadith*, or traditions, of the Prophet. They prescribe a place for the horse as part of the religious obligations of a Muslim, reminding the faithful that "the blessings of this world shall hang from the forelocks between your horses' eyes until Judgment Day," and then "a horse's hunger and thirst, the water he drinks, the food he eats, every hair on the animal, the least step he takes, and even his urine and dung will be weighed in the balance."

಼

Arabs were racing horses before the time of Muhammad, and traditional training regimens at one time included a fattening on grain followed by a forty-day fast, at the beginning of which the horses were covered with seven blankets, with one removed every six days, and increasing exercise. Races were run in fields of ten, with the first seven being rewarded. Nowadays, wherever Thoroughbreds race, the heritage of Arab horses is always present; over 90 percent of them trace their descent from the Darley Arabian.

There is no equestrian culture in which horse racing has not played a part. The Scythians indulged in it, the Mongols reveled in it, the Greeks and the Romans institutionalized it. The plains Indians seem to have started horse racing as soon as they began horseback riding (and among the Blackfoot, races were held soon after that old mallard turned into a horse). The races were long, as far as one could see on the open plain, which would have made them about the same length—four miles and up—as racecourses common in Europe and the United States during the seventeenth and eighteenth centuries, and a winning racehorse was a valuable commodity. Like all players of games, the Blackfoot liked to set up a small, unlikely looking horse whose appearance belied its speed and stamina against a larger, more elegant one, in order to raise the stakes. Watching their boys riding colts and chasing buffalo calves, they would select the best colts, taking them aside and training them until they were ready to run at three or four years.

Then they would put them into competition at seasonal camps and at Sun Dance ceremonies in late summer, and occasionally the best were put against the best of other tribes in match races, though traditional hostilities often interfered.

The first horse race in England of which we have a record was during Roman times (in 208 CE); but there would have been races much earlier, simply because horses were there. In modern times, in the United States and Canada as well as in Europe and South America, racing became a major industry. Australians began racing in

1821—the Melbourne Cup is now a classic—and the Irish have become one of the world's great breeders of race-horses and jumpers.

And this just gets us to the starting gate, and only with Thoroughbreds. Other racing traditions thrive, such as the Quarter-horse races in the United States, run over a quarter mile because that was about the length of the main street in the Old West (the considerable width of the streets, on the other hand, was designed to let a mule team turn around). And harness racing has a large following and a long history—both with trotters (who run with one foreleg and the opposite hind leg off the ground at the same time) and pacers (who have a lateral gait, with both legs on each side on or off the ground).

⟞

Except for public executions and gladiatorial spectacles, horse racing was probably the preeminent competitive sport in terms of public interest until prizefighting and team sports like football took over. And for many of us, the enduring image of it is the jockey riding high on the back of a thundering Thoroughbred, heels down in short stirrups while sitting—or standing—forward in his seat. It wasn't always so for jockeys. Until the American Tod Sloan, riding in England in 1897, demonstrated the advantages of short stirrups and the forward seat—in what was unkindly called the "monkey crouch," or "monkey up a stick"—riders in Europe and the United States sat much more upright, with their weight correspondingly further back. Sloan said he had learned to ride his way from the Sioux. He could have; or from the Arabs, or the nomads of the steppes. He certainly helped usher in a new era in modern riding, and even became the subject of two memorable show tunes, "Yankee Doodle Dandy" and "Give My Regards to Broadway."

The fascination of racing is not simply the competition itself, and the money to be won—or lost—by placing a bet. But that certainly has enormous appeal, and it became big business after a man named Joseph Oller, who won a bet in a pool but was not paid at the French Grand Prix in 1864, invented a system that he distinguished from the regular pools by calling it "pari-mutuel" betting (*pari* being a word of his invention, from *parier*, to bet).

This was an era when there was a lot of money in racing, first of all money to be spent on breeding and training and care. So the owners of racehorses were often wealthy, for a while at least, and often of noble lineage, just as they hoped their horses would turn out to be. Royal patronage of a serious sort began in England with Henry VIII and continued until the execution of Charles I (though Cromwell himself, a military man, was also an enthusiastic breeder of horses). With the restoration of the monarchy in 1660, Charles II returned horse racing to its rightful place, even riding a winner himself at Newmarket in 1671. Increasingly, he paid more attention to the racing turf than to the state of the realm, setting a precedent that was later embellished by men of wealth and clout like the 5th Earl of Roseberry, whose horse won the Derby twice in a row —in 1894 and 1895—while he was the prime minister. Some narrow-minded individuals thought he should turn his energies rather more to governing the country.

Derby Day in England has always been a great occasion, and in 1895 it was one of the first sporting events to be filmed (just shortly after Eadweard Muybridge had made history with his photographs). The following year, in 1896, Robert Paul—who was already well known for his "Theatrograph" moving pictures—was commissioned by London's Alhambra Music Hall to film the Derby. This time it was won by Persimmon, a horse owned by the Prince of

Wales (who became Edward VII). Paul had the two-and-a-half-minute show ready for viewing the following evening.

British music halls and racetracks, like Roman circuses and Broadway theaters, were in the entertainment business. So they built them larger, and—in the case of racetracks—ironically relied on a railway system that had replaced horse transportation to bring in large crowds. Betting was the key, and in its wake an expanding sporting press to supply the demand for news and views. The racetrack became a place to be reckoned with. In 1913, again at the running of the Derby, King Edward VII's horse Amner was in the lead coming round Tottenham Corner when Emily Davison—a fanatic member of the Women's Social and Political Union—slipped under the rails and threw herself in front of the horse, bringing Amner and his jockey, Herbert Jones, tumbling to the turf. Afterwards, in great anxiety the king asked after his horse and jockey. The horse was alright, the jockey was hurt. But Miss Davison was dead. The suffragettes had another martyr.

❧

There are other great traditions of horse racing, many of them derived from the hunt and practiced for ages, like steeplechasing—named after a race in 1752 between the steeples of Buttevant Church and St. Leger Church in County Cork in Ireland—or racing over obstacles, natural or not. It was institutionalized in Europe in the eighteenth century, though it had its counterpart in the formalized jumping and dressage of the great riding schools. Later, there came the daring horse and chariot—a.k.a. chuckwagon—races that were part of many rodeos. Showing its kinship with the circus, the word "rodeo" comes from the Spanish *rodear*, to go round; and a turn at a rodeo event is still called a "go-round."

When it comes to competition on horseback, there are many connections across cultures. A game called *pato*, played from the early seventeenth century in Argentina, in which riders fought for the possession of a duck that was killed and stuffed into a hide, had similarities with the buzkashi of the Afghans and Mongols. Pato eventually became a dangerous cross-country free-for-all, and was banned in 1822; when it was reinstated in the 1930s, it was as a modern regulated sport played on a large field, 90 by 230 yards.

Wrestling on horseback has been popular for thousands of years, formalized among the herdsmen of the steppes into a game called *sais*. The gauchos of Argentina and the *huasos* of Chile have a game of "crowding" on horseback, in which the riders try to push each other's horses off the track. Closer to a tournament, and with Arab origins, is a form of jousting in South America where a rider, going full tilt towards his opponent, throws a cane at him, the trick being to catch the cane without being hit by it. And there is the ring race, popular in medieval Spain and still run in the Americas, in which a rider at top speed tries to skewer a tiny dangling ring with a lance. The games of the gymkhana, begun as training exercises by Indian cavalry during British colonial days and now popular across the United States and in Great Britain, run the gamut from a "keyhole" competition, where riders have to negotiate a narrow passage and tight turn, to barrel racing and "pick-up" competitions, in which a rider going at full gallop (and sometimes bareback) tries to pick up a small object from the ground.

The signal competition linking ancient and modern worlds are the Olympic Games. Horses—the only animals participating in the Olympics—were introduced to the modern games in 1912 in an event called the "military"; the name was later changed to the "three-day event," and it really came into its own after World War I. For a couple of decades most of the competitors were cavalry officers and their mounts, reflecting an old practice among equestrian peoples all over the world of using trials such as this to test themselves and their horses. But civilians soon participated as well, and the three-day event has become the preeminent competition for horse and rider, incorporating cross-country (with speed, endurance, and steeplechase segments), dressage, and show jumping.

Women played an important part in this equestrian transformation. Alone among Olympic events, and rare enough anywhere in the world of sports, the modern games have brought women in to compete on an equal footing—or seating—against the men. No special considerations, no shorter fairways, no head starts. Whoever rides best, man or woman, wins. Sure enough, women have won medals, including Olympic gold, against the men.

⤜

It is easy to say that there is nothing complicated about a sporting event like a horse race; but just tell that to the tens of thousands of people who go watch them every day, and who try to figure out how to place their bets. On the other hand, the tradition that produced the great schools of equitation of Europe seem at first glance very complicated. And yet *its* goal, at least in the late nineteenth and early twentieth centuries, was simplicity.

Equitation training originally came out of military traditions, and at the end of the nineteenth century it had reached a crisis. It wasn't just that the role of the horse in the wider society, as well as in war, was uncertain at this time. This crisis went deeper—and as so often with horses, it was formal as well as functional. It had to do with a conflict between naturalness and artifice.

After wandering and settling down, it's the oldest argument in the history of humanity. But it had taken a new

Training of cavalry horses in front of the Vienna Arsenal barracks (ca. 1850)

turn with modern military strategy. Cavalry training at the time emphasized jumping, along with various other moves on the flat, to prepare rider and horse for the cavalry charge. That was the ultimate end of the training. But the future—brief though it would be—was in a cavalry that could move swiftly and safely over all terrain, a return to the light horsemen of the steppes.

Europe's cavalry schools—except for the British ones—did not participate in hunts, so they were bound into routines that did not prepare for that kind of riding. And since civilians had no say in those schools, nobody was there to temper the nostalgia of the officers for the old days of the dashing charge. The main cavalry schools were in France (at Fontainbleau, Versailles, and Saumur), Austria (in Vienna), and Germany (in Munich and Hanover), their methods inherited from the older tradition of haute école.

Of course, many of the great practitioners of the time maintained an elegant middle way between reining in and releasing their horses to do whatever was required. But a broader theory of the relationship between horse and rider, appropriate to the demands of a modern cavalry, had yet to be established.

The problem was in part a theoretical one—the question whether jumping comes naturally to a horse. Many argued that it did not, since a horse in a field with a relatively low fence will not normally jump over it (unless frightened into doing so). And a horse's bodily structure, unlike that of a dog or an elk, is not really designed for jumping, with relatively inefficient leverage for takeoff (horses have more ribs than dogs and cats, which makes it harder for them to draw their hindquarters under) and poorly designed shock absorbers for landing (paws are much better than hoofs).

But others saw jumping as natural, or at least learnable within a framework in which the horse is not asked to do anything that doesn't come agreeably to it. One of these was an Italian army officer by the name of Federico Caprilli, who established a modern tradition by recovering an ancient one, blending Mongol and Mogul and Arab elements with contemporary military practice. And in a wonderful irony, Caprilli's approach became the single most important inspiration for teaching riders and training horses in peacetime, as a natural and relatively gentle tradition of riding emerged out of the unnatural brutality of war.

Caprilli was born into a wealthy Italian family and entered the cavalry training school in 1886 (the year my grandfather met Crop Eared Wolf). Indeed, Caprilli's influence coincided with the threat to the plains Indian equestrian tradition with which it had so much in common. As the Blackfoot watched the end of an era, Caprilli saw the beginning of another. And he changed the way people rode.

At the time, Caprilli did not seem the ideal physical type for the cavalry—his back was long and his legs were short—and so the military school medical board initially rejected him. But an opening came up, and he was grudgingly admitted.

He excelled, especially at jumping, which was the centerpiece of equestrian education then. At the Turin International Jumping Trials in 1902—a prelude to the introduction of equestrian competition into the Olympic Games—Caprilli and his horse astounded everyone by jumping a record height of 2.08 meters and a record long jump of 7.40 meters. As his natural talents took him into technical innovations, his imagination and intelligence made him stand back and think about what exactly was going on when a horse and rider went over a jump. It wasn't that nobody had thought about this before; but they had thought about it only in relation to a style that emphasized the rider's elegance, alternately sitting in the saddle or standing in the stirrups and maintaining control by collecting the horse, with constant pressure on the mouth.

Caprilli proposed a method that brought the rider into closer touch with a horse's physical capabilities and mental instincts. Naturalness was its watchword. Simplicity was its virtue. "Natural equitation," he called it, to distinguish it from "school equitation." School equitation had, and still has, remarkable achievements; and the riders at renowned centers such as Vienna's Spanish Riding School display an understanding of their horses that is the product of a life-time of training. But the difference is fundamental. In school equitation, the horse is trained to adapt to the rider; in natural equitation, the rider adapts to the horse. Instead of pounding a horse's loins and dragging on his mouth, Caprilli tried for a deft touch, a light seat, and immediate response, like a cowboy cutting cattle on a horse.

Caprilli watched horses from the ground up, studying the way they moved at every gait and then while jumping (. . . and he fell onto the ground so many times while try-ing out his techniques that once he had to take six months off to recover). One of the things he recognized—which seemed to have eluded many other riders—was that a horse has remarkable eyes, able to detect movement and to identify objects and individuals at great distances. And horses can see in almost every direction, 340 out of 360 degrees. But they *do* have two blind spots: directly behind —and directly in front. And because of the placement of their eyes, horses also have poor depth perception. If a horse's head is held high going into a jump, she cannot gauge the ground nor see the jump. Natural or not, jumping turned out to be the perfect place to start thinking about how horses and riders could cooperate.

Caprilli's focus was on the field rather than the arena or the track, for horses were still an essential part of the military. In theory, his reforms were designed to maintain and strengthen conservative principles of horsemanship; in practice, they prepared the horse and rider to be ready for change. Perhaps not by chance, it was also at this time that the other great education reforms of the twentieth century began, proposed by the likes of Maria Montessori and Rudolf Steiner.

By the time he died in 1907, Caprilli's method was used by the entire Italian cavalry, with demonstrations of its success continuing to be made in a variety of surprising ways. His influence—spread in part by Piero Santini, who wrote with passionate conviction about Caprilli's work—flowed to the great equestrian schools in Poland and Hungary, France, and England, and (by way of Hungary and Italy) to the United States.

So the horse had come full circle, not only back to the Americas but home from the battlefield to the show ring. Once again, she was a domestic animal to be ridden by boys and girls and men and women who did not want to or could not be expected to dedicate their entire lives to a horse. Federico Caprilli opened the stable doors, clearing away the association of the horse with aristocratic (and military) privilege.

Keeping a horse still costs money, more or less depending on where you live, so not everyone can afford one, not by a long shot. But since horses have become less essential for transportation and communication, riding has taken a new role in many of our cultures. In the 1980s, a rough census of horses worldwide put the number at 167 million. Most of those were ridden for pleasure.

The past century has seen both a democratization of the horse, and a new domestication of her. And the place most horses these days are looked after, and loved, and where they learn a great deal about the ways of the world they must live in is—the barn.

꿿

From yurts and teepees to sod huts and brick houses, and from stone castles and glass mansions to thatched cottages and timbered homes, humans have sheltered themselves from the weather, raised families, and brought friends together in *buildings*. The one thing that all these buildings have in common is that they are discovered, devised, or designed by humans. Just like barns, they are the product of ingenious artifice. Humans need shelter, just as they need food and water, and even more than that they need each other. But horses have different needs. Horses eat and drink, as we do, and they sleep, though not nearly as much and mostly at different times; and while they prefer company, like us, they too can do without it. But unlike humans, horses live naturally in the open, moving about, seeking shelter in coulees or under the cottonwood trees.

Domesticating horses meant making new dwelling places for them. At first, these would have been hills and valleys with natural barriers to keep the horses from wandering, and out of the wind; and then fenced corrals or makeshift and movable bivouacs. At some point, in some circumstances, humans would have built barns.

Barns were always a human convenience, not a way of making a horse happier. Some horses have taken to barns; but basically, a barn is an unnatural place for a horse to be. The Arabs, like the plains Indians, preferred to keep horses in the open, though they made sure—often at considerable cost to their own comfort—that there was natural shelter nearby, and of course water.

But the open range is not an option for most of us, so we build barns. Barns turn wanderers into settlers, which is what civilization always tries to do, pretending that it is

Winter in Connecticut (George Henry Durrie, ca. 1858)

a natural evolution. We naturalize barns just as we naturalize towns and cities.

This has been part of the history of humans and horses from the beginning. But it does create problems for both. The problems for people, crowding into cities, are well documented; the problems for horses, like cribbing (biting onto the stable rack or manger and sucking air) and weaving (nervously rocking side to side), are well known to horse people—and they call them "vices." In good barns much effort is put into trying to persuade horses that this is the natural place for them to be. Horses know better. But they also know how to adapt.

From a horse's point of view, the most annoying thing about barns is that they are boring. And the most successful barns aren't built of this or that material, or designed in this way or that (though there are of course good and bad buildings), but are places in which certain rituals, certain social—some would say spiritual—ceremonies are established and maintained. In a magical way, this seems to keep the humans as well as the horses happy.

The rituals have to do with feeding and watering, cleaning and grooming, breeding and birthing, training and talking. Just as they do for us. And perhaps not sur-

prisingly, those rituals that are the epitome of human artifice soon become the most natural of habits. In the old
days, when you learned a language—surely the most
unnatural thing we do—the saying was that you "had the
habit of it." Barn rituals are a language, a habit; and they go
a long way toward making the barn—which is the horse's
house—into a home.

The barn I remember best, other than the one in which
I raised my own horses, stood in southern Ontario. It was
owned by Reg Greer, a great breeder of hunters and
jumpers, some of them carrying the Canadian colors to the
Olympics. It was built of big old cedar logs, straight as a
die and strong as steel and still smelling sweet a hundred
years after they were set down on top of the fieldstone
foundations, with siding of rough milled planks long
since gone gray, but better than almost anything we have
come up with since. Like all living things, these logs and
planks breathed.

Reg liked rituals, and he knew that horses liked them
too. Most of these were part of an everyday mealtime
routine, with certain horses being on different diets, and

occasionally different schedules. After feeding he would let them out into the paddock, watching how they went along and got along; and after he had cleaned their stalls and done a dozen other chores he would let them in again and talk to them in tones that varied according to their individual dispositions rather than his own mood (which, truth be told, was not without its ups and downs).

Afterwards, down the alley between the two-year-olds where he kept his tack, and surrounded by a great audience in the stalls, Reg would sit and talk. It was always dark in there, and the sweet-smelling hay bales piled over by the grain bin cut the cold that always came up from the concrete floor put down thirty years before, and in the winter came down from the beams that held up the threshing floor and hay mow above.

The stalls were set down on both sides of the ground floor of the barn, and were built of twelve- to fifteen-inch cedar planks, thick as a wrist. There were stalls out in the pole barn too, joined to the main barn by a grain silo, and at the far end, beyond the big doors that opened onto the barnyard and the paddock, was a separate shed where Tamarack, Reg's famous stallion, was installed.

There was a medicine cabinet in the barn—an old

bathroom cupboard nailed to one of the cedar beams—where Reg kept some mineral oil and aloes for dosing a colicky horse, borax and silver nitrate for nerves (the horses', that is), a knife for cleaning hoofs, pincers and pliers for more serious business, instructions for the new mower, and a bottle of whisky for miscellaneous crises and celebrations (Reg's, that is).

Some old horse collars hung on the walls. An old sled break, a heavy iron staple forged by a blacksmith at a time when there still was one nearby, sat on a shelf behind some liniment over the grain bin; and behind it an old picture of a Hackney horse driving an elegant carriage—one foreleg picked up, neck arched high, eyes looking over at the camera to make sure it is catching how pretty she is, bred and born right there by Reg, then raised and shown with a batch of blue ribbons pinned underneath to tell the story of their success. Reg's achievement was his horses.

To a background of snorts and nickers and the lovely soft blowing sound that horses make when things are fine, he would talk about horses. And it was their ritual too, for he would only talk about them where they could hear him. Reg didn't talk about horses the way he talked about other things—like baseball, which he loved; or his boys,

with whom he had epic battles; or his neighbors, who had
been his neighbors all his life, and all his father's and his
grandfather's and his great-grandfather's too, right from the
time when they had all come from the north of Ireland to
settle in Ontario's Mulmur Hills in the 1830s and 1840s
and brought their knowledge of horses with them. Hunger
didn't haunt them, as it did some of their kin. But horses
did, and a heritage of bittersweet independence.

Reg didn't talk about horses as though they were
people, though he sometimes talked about people as
though they were horses. Horses were horses. They spoke
differently, they listened differently, they watched things
differently, and they thought differently. Like him. He
liked to go over to look at a horse as he talked, even when
he wasn't talking about that particular horse. It had something to do with a sense of solidarity in that secret society,
that secret language, of horses and horsepeople. But Reg
was not a whisperer. Few horse whisperers are.

He had worked with horses from the time he could
walk. When he was fourteen, his father died and Reg left
school to run the family farm, the farm he lived on all his
life. He had the patience of a peasant, the faith of a farmer,
and the toughness of a horse trader. As the market for

horses changed and Hackneys, which were once the sports cars of the horse world, became less popular he turned to hunters and jumpers, the SUVs of equestrian folk. And buyers came to his old-fashioned farm from all over the world.

Electricity only arrived in 1952, and that was good, because it meant safe lights in the barn. Tractors came around the same time; but Reg had grown up working the fields with horses, and he could not imagine being without them. He treated his tractors like working stock, acknowledging their personalities and wary of their power; but tractors were designed to do what they were told. He loved how horses were determined to surprise him.

Reg also loved horses because they bound him to that place. They were household gods, long-memoried and short-tempered, mostly good but occasionally tramps and tricksters. You could never leave them alone. Reg had not been off the farm for more than a day or two for twenty-five years. Horses needed watching. They let you wander, but they made you settle down.

This was where humans and horses began, on the family farm. It hadn't always looked this way; but it had always felt like this. Reg's Irish ancestry put him and his horses in line with a horse culture that stretched back to the beginnings of time, and reunited the horse breeds of northern Mongolia and Europe with those of southwestern Asia and the Middle East, all fellow travelers across the Bering Land Bridge way back when.

Chapter 6

THE SPIRIT OF HORSES

Power, Grace, and Beauty

Most of us have two images of a horse. Between them lies the history of humanity.

One is the workhorse, which includes the plow horse, the horse drawing a cart, the family horse upon whom generations rode to school, the stable horse that young children work and play with on the weekend, the horse that we see in the showring or at the racetrack, the horse on the polo field or in the circus, the horse in carvings and sculptures and friezes and vases from ancient times—pulling kings and gods in chariots or carrying them, or just standing in a noble pose—and the horse in paintings from the Paleolithic to the postmodern and in photographic images from Muybridge to the movies.

And then there is the image of a horse running free across the steppes of Russia or the marshlands of the Camargue in France or the prairies of the Americas or the moors of the British Isles or the dunes of Sable Island off Nova Scotia or the outback of Australia. The wild horse. The horse we used to slaughter, and now we want to save.

In between is the horse described by Carl R. Raswan at the beginning of *Drinkers of the Wind*, a book about Arab horses. "He was an impatient creature with quivering limbs. His eyes flashed fiery light. His nostrils flared defiance. He tossed his head upon a lofty neck. His carriage was noble and his shape handsome, set upon the most tender feet. He hung in an old stained cedar frame above my bed."

❧

This book is full of workhorses—and the in-between ones, from Black Beauty to My Friend Flicka, and from the earliest cave art to the latest posters and calendars. Many of the people we know best, and care for most, are the people we meet in books. It's the same with horses. Books and pictures. Some of our most memorable horses are those we know only in our imaginations.

Much of our attention these days is upon wild horses, the wanderers of the horse world. Like the nomads of the steppes, they represent something important in the history of both horses and humans, each wandering for tens of thousands of years in a world shaped by the other.

By bringing horses into the sphere of civilization, and using them to hunt and herd other animals, humans may have saved them from extinction in those ancient days when the savannah lands were being taken over by forests, and predators lay waiting. But when we fenced them in fields, installed them in stables, bred them for function and fancy, and surrounded them with our sense of community, they could only dream of the mountains and the rivers that once surrounded them on the great plains of Asia and the Americas. And so could we. There is a story about a tribal chief in India thousands of years ago who let his horses graze free for twelve months. Then he decided that the limit of his home, and of theirs, would be determined by wherever they had roamed that year. "O give me a home, where the wild horses roam. . . ."

What we now call wild horses are nothing of the kind. They are the descendants of runaways, horses that left humans to go walkabout in the wilderness, returning to the old, old fight against their natural enemies—big cats and dogs, and the climate. One word for them is "feral"; but it's gotten a bad rap. Some prefer to call such horses "maroons," from the Spanish *cimarron*, meaning wild, though this term has its own complexity. Maroon was the name taken by enslaved people who escaped the sugar plantations of the Caribbean and South America and established communities

Wild Horses at Play (George Catlin, 1834–1837)

in remote terrain in the centuries following 1492; it reflects their fierce dedication to freedom and their equally fierce defense of their own territory.

Like the civilized and the barbaric, the wild and the tame are arbitrary categories. So is HORSE itself, a category cobbled together from scraps of hair and bits of bone by paleontologists and archaeologists and zoologists and other natural historians. Two hundred years ago, the theory of evolution was inspired by horse bones and a fossil memory taking us back to the dawn of time. Almost every week brings a new pile of bones, in a new place, to turn our theories upside down. Horses stride across the old worlds of Asia, Africa, and Europe, and they seem to have been in the Americas since time immemorial. Which is five hundred years, and ten thousand, and fifty million.

As biological categories go, HORSE may hold together only by the skin of its teeth, but it allows us to distinguish horses from asses and zebras, all three of which belong to the genus *equus*. It also makes it clear that a horse is something more than a donkey with floppy ears, or a zebra without the stripes.

Before they took to horses, humans domesticated donkeys, which are descendants of the wild African asses. The sibling species are the Asiatic asses, which once wandered the deserts and steppes from Syria to Mongolia, often in very large groups; they were hunted and herded, and occasionally harnessed, but they were hard to train. Donkeys, on the other hand, could be used relatively easily for riding and carrying and pulling, though they lacked the speed and strength of horses. But they didn't overeat or overheat the way horses did, which meant that they weren't nearly as susceptible to colic, and could go much longer without food and water. So they had a useful place in human society, while Asiatic asses were hunted out of the territory, and some of their subspecies (like onagers) almost out of existence. Being inveterate tinkerers, humans bred horses and donkeys and produced the mule; and the mule was put to work before horses were.

The zebras were even more standoffish than the asses, and were never domesticated the way horses and donkeys were; during the rainy season they still congregate on the Serengeti-Mara plains in herds of over 10,000. But over the years they have been hunted extensively for their flesh and skins; one of four species of zebras, the Quagga, is now extinct, and several subspecies are in jeopardy.

Do wild horses really represent the essence of HORSE, from a time before agriculture and settlement closed in, when the horse herd ran free? Has the domesticated horse fallen from grace by going into gardening? Is a civilized horse a kind of corrupted horse, and the wild horse the noble primitive? However we see it, there is an eerie similarity between this line of argument and that which was applied to native Americans, that the settling down and "civilizing"—or domestication—of them meant the end of their aboriginal state, the destruction of their "true" identity. But just as the Indians of the plains didn't become any less Indian when they took up horses and guns— indeed, many might say they became more themselves— so horses didn't become any less HORSE when they took up with humans.

Still, the idea of the vanishing "wild" Indian was a staple of the early twentieth century, just as the vanishing of the untamed horse is of ours. And along with this goes a sense that the native horse, like the native people, both must be saved yet cannot possibly be saved. For some reason, humans seem to savor this contradiction. All of this is premised on an ideal in which purity is synonymous with the primitive, and the civilized with the corrupt.

This book suggests a different view, one that has more to do with horses. The civilized horse, the workhorse, is a horse in parenthesis. The wild horse is a horse in quotation marks. Together, they make up what we think of as HORSE.

And this is how horses help us. They embody the in-between, not only in between wandering and settling down but also in between the fenced and the free. "I don't want to get adjusted to this world anymore," say horses and humans, in the words of the old Baptist hymn. And then they do.

Still, the ideal of that idyllic place, on the plains or the pampas or the savannahs or the steppes where horses roamed free and found their true home, haunts us like Eden, even though we know that it was a perilous place, where horses might not have survived their natural predators, including us. But now that the genuinely "wild" horses, horses that have never been domesticated, seem to be gone from these lands, the maroons provide us with a connection to our shared past, which is why they decorate our walls and disturb our consciences. For the wild horse is, in a sense, a domestic invention, giving us a way of imagining what it would be like to be free and to wander with the herd in the field of our dreams.

～

If we value wild horses so much, why would we take pleasure and even pride in our ability to tame them, as Monty Roberts famously tamed a wild horse called Shy Boy? Because we can—or more precisely, because he can?

Perhaps. But most of all it probably has to do with something much deeper in human consciousness, something connected to the strength it takes to surrender, and the generosity of spirit a horse displays when he does so. It's a gift of grace, a form of forgiveness; and when a wild horse is tamed, or a young horse is trained, we take custody of that gift and catch a glimpse of that generosity. And we know we need it in our world, to learn from and live by. That might be the most important lesson of Shy Boy. It's a lesson we learn, too, when we watch a horse pulling a plow, or hauling logs, or showing her paces in the ring, or running round the track.

Maybe our fascination with horses began with what comes naturally to them, like finding their way home in the dark. It has to do with their eyes, of course, which have a special membrane that reflects light back onto the retina, so they glow like night-vision goggles. But there is something else, even more mysterious. As migrating birds find their way home across continents and oceans, year after year, and salmon return from the sea to spawn in the very same river where they were born, so horses seem to have a special homing instinct. Perhaps they follow magnetic fields across unfamiliar terrain, as birds do; or they could be guided by smell, as salmon probably are. But whatever the case, it is amazing.

Or did we become fascinated with horses when they fulfilled one of our oldest dreams, flying in the air even as they remained earthbound, just like us?

Maybe it had to do with horses being unpredictable, mischievous and malicious by turns, like the Greek gods.

Or maybe it was that sometimes, when they came into view, the world seemed to stand still for a moment—and so did they, even when they were running free. Some of the greatest artists in the world have tried to catch that hovering moment between the earth and the air, between force and finesse, between the canyon and the corral, and their attempts continue to enthrall us.

*Head of one of the four
horses from St. Mark's
Basilica in Venice*

One magnificent example is the four bronze horses crowning the main entrance of St. Mark's Basilica in Venice, probably cast in the fourth century BCE by Lysippos, the only sculptor Alexander the Great would allow to do his portrait. These horses were originally brought to Rome by Nero, where they stayed until his death in 68 CE. They reappeared 250 years later in Constantinople, where Constantine took them to stand atop the starting gates at his chariot-racing Hippodrome. When the Crusaders sacked the city in the early thirteenth century, they took the horses back to the Doge of Venice, who had funded their sea voyage in exchange for booty. There they stayed until Napoleon herded them off to Paris and set them on top of the Arc du Carroussel, at the opposite end of the Champs Elysées from the Arc de Triomphe, to celebrate his victories. But the 1815 Congress of Vienna returned them to Venice, where they have remained (apart from a few visits to safe houses during the two World Wars, and a later international exhibition tour). Even bronze horses are constantly on the move, occasionally get stolen, and live a life in between wandering and settling down.

Our world of art is full of horses, from the cave paintings at Chauvet and the portrait of Whistlejacket to the photographic images of Secretariat or Seabiscuit thundering to the finish line. It includes the ethereal Chinese "Flying Horse," cast in bronze in the second century CE, the carved wooden horse effigies of the plains Indians, the wonderful abstract swirl of Franz Marc's horses (one of the members of the expressionist artists' group Der Blaue Reiter, or The Blue Rider), and the oriental sweep of Frank Mechau's ponies, painted on murals throughout Colorado and the West during the 1930s and 1940s. For millennia, artists around the world have tried to catch this singular moment between motion and rest. It's like trying to catch a spirit, which is what the arts are always trying to do, and why horses have so often been their subject.

It is also what religion is all about; and horses have had their place in many of the world's great spiritual traditions, as tombs and other testimonials remind us. There have been haunting images of horses throughout history, from the Celtic figure of a horse with a human head in the fifth century BCE to the *kinnaras* of ancient India two thousand years earlier, where a man's head was replaced with that of a horse (often linked with birds and music in an Asian version of the Blackfoot legend of the mallard-horse). Some myths of origin have other features in common: Pegasus, the winged horse of Greek mythology, for example, was born of the Gorgon Medusa's blood, while in the Norse world of the gods Odin's horse, Sleipnir, was the offspring of the evil Loki—when he turned himself into a mare—and Svaldifari, the horse of the Giants. Imaginary horses that combine both the dark and the light side of life . . .

Impossible beings, with impossible (and in some cases, deeply disturbing) provenance. But like many impossible and disturbing things, people believed in them. Even the physician Galen, who treated Marcus Aurelius and was an exemplar of ancient rationality, argued about whether the bile of a centaur relieved apoplexy; if no one had believed in centaurs, or horse medicine, he wouldn't have had the argument. And horses have been bound into belief in other ways, with words for "horse" and "mind" being close cousins in many ancient languages. From the nomadic peoples of the central steppes to the charioteers of the Middle East, from the Islamic horse culture to the Christian chevaliers, and from the plains Indians of the Americas to the riding schools of modern Europe, horses represented the search for control over the uncontrollable, which is one reason they were often invoked to portray the paradox of religion, and the relationships between the natural and the supernatural that myth explores.

Myth also makes sense of contradictions, if only for a moment; and it is a response to human curiosity, that ambivalent virtue that both settles and unsettles us. The products of our curiosity, like fire and language and the hunting tools that gave early humans the ability to exercise dominion over so much land, have often been credited with spiritual or supernatural power. So it should come as no surprise that horses were revered, for they both deciphered and deepened the mystery of life. The

Mongol word for horse, the center of their everyday lives, is *takh*, which means spirit.

For millennia, horses have shaped belief and provided consolation. The World Tree of Norse mythology, a giant ash tree, was called Yggdrasil, meaning "The Terrible One's Horse," and it was there that the gods held their congregations. And horses inspired the holy book of Zoroaster, the *Zend Avesta*, which is filled with references to horse-worshiping heroes. Epona, the Celtic horse-goddess whose daughter was Gaul, was taken up by the Roman cavalry as a spirit of that place; and, probably in honor of her British incarnation Rhiannon, the great white horse of Uffington—about 365 feet long—was cut out of the turf on a hillside in the Berkshire Downs over 2,500 years ago. The story continues all over the world, with horses snorting and snickering in sacred woods and on the wide-open steppes and in the skies and under the soil throughout the ages.

Like gods, these horses are more human than human beings—and they are not human at all. They are made in our own image, and sometimes it seems we are made in theirs. They are vindictive and virtuous by turns, quiet and cantankerous, strong and fearless in the presence of danger and frightened by a rabbit and laid low by a stomachache. They seldom complain, and they always let their feelings be known. We can explain some of this, but we don't want to. Horses are spirit made flesh, and like all spirits and things of the flesh, they baffle us. But they also call on our respect. One of Muhammad's rituals was to wipe his horse's eyes and nostrils as a sign of respect.

The trainer Buck Brannaman, famous for his work with both horses and riders and as a stand-in for Robert Redford in the film *The Horse Whisperer*, wrote a book whose title catches both the romance and the reality. It's called *The Faraway Horses*, because that's the phrase his children used to describe why he was out wandering and away from home for such long periods. In fact, he was holding clinics and helping people understand how to work with horses, how to communicate with them, how to call upon their generosity of spirit (especially when they were biting and kicking). But in his children's fancy—and in his, too—Buck was visiting those faraway horses.

These same horses bring us home, and come into our languages with "bits and pieces"—a phrase that originally had to do with a horse's bridle—with "horseplay" and "horse sense" and "putting on airs" and "putting the cart before the horse" and "starting from scratch" and "giving someone a leg up" and "riding roughshod" over them . . . a "dark horse candidate," perhaps, one who was "champing at the bit" but needed to "get off his high horse" and stop "tilting at windmills."

These faraway horses enter our dreams, too, and they provide common ground across cultures as different as ancient Asia and modern Europe, hunting societies and agricultural ones, rural and urban dwellers, in war and peace. Riding is both the most unnatural thing for a human to do and the most natural. Horses are both a walk in the storm and a shelter from it, and they take us closer to the world by taking us further away.

They also defy our categories, so that we are never sure of the difference between cause and effect. The philosopher Herbert Simon tells about watching an ant work its way along a beach. The surface is uneven, and the ingenuity of the ant in navigating across it is wonderful to behold. Except that the wonder, Simon suggests, might just as properly be in the beach rather than the ant. Viewed that way, it is the beach that is complex; the ant is just an ant, barely sophisticated enough to use the beach to find its way. Humans and horses may be like that ant and that beach, something all the great horse cultures of the world have acknowledged in one way or another.

꩜

Big Bird was seventeen when she came out of the mountains in the spring of 1933. Later that year, after a brief stretch in a makeshift corral that Bobby Attachie put together from split cedar rails (which a homesteader had left when he picked up and went back to Vancouver after that godawful winter), eating hay that Mindy Christiansen had gotten for them, she had a long spell down in Bumpy Meadows, where there was alfalfa and clover. And now she was looking good.

So good that things began to happen. She had had five foals already, so she knew the signs. Bobby had borrowed a stallion from a fellow up the way who was farming where his grandfather, Jerry Attachie, used to set his summer camp, right by a nice little creek that gurgled away winter and summer, fed by a spring and the snow in the mountains.

Rupert was the stallion's name. He wasn't a real looker, but like all good stallions, he was always looking for the next town. And he could swap in like a swallow, turning on a dime and giving you change.

Bobby rode Rupert down to where they had their camp. When he got there, Rupert didn't pay any mind to Big Bird. So Bobby put him over by the woods in the corral at one end of Bumpy Meadows, with Big Bird grazing at the other about a half mile away. Two days later, Rupert scrunched up his nose and bared his teeth in what looked like a grin. He was ready. Or more accurately, Big Bird was ready. She was winking at him, even at that distance.

So Bobby pulled down a couple of poles to open the corral gate. There was a pounding of hoofs as Rupert came by for a closer look; then a noisy bit of sniffing, some nickering sweet talk, a nibble or two on her neck—the nibble marks were still there a month later—and a whinny that sounded like he was about to crash into something.

Sex doesn't take long for a horse. Horses are like teenagers where sex is concerned—they always seem to be scared of getting caught. Panic comes naturally to them. So it all takes place in under a minute.

Wanting to make it last a little longer, Big Bird and Rupert did it a half dozen more times over the next few weeks. Of course, Rupert did a lot of other things during that time, and he did a lot of other mares. But Big Bird got to recognize his nicker. Once, she wasn't in the mood, and when Rupert came behind her and started to nibble her neck, she kicked him. He backed off and came back the next day.

Sure enough, Big Bird got pregnant, and later that summer, Bobby took her down south to trade. He didn't want to let her go; but he knew that she would be worth something now, and they were trying to build up the herd. She would have her foal next spring, eleven months later.

Things had changed down by the Milk River ridge where Bobby took Big Bird and where Crop Eared Wolf had lived fifty years earlier. A road had gone through the country, and the Blackfoot had moved to the towns that had sprung up around. Crop Eared Wolf had died the year after the first Calgary Stampede, seeing the beginning of the next chapter in the long history of horses and humans. He was succeeded as head chief by Shot in Both Sides. Many had hoped it would be Wolf Moccasin, who was also known as Joe Healy.

Healy had been adopted by a white family after his parents had been killed in a raid by the Pend d'Oreille Indians down in Montana, and so was raised between two worlds. He was deeply traditional, one of the few Kainai not to convert to Christianity; but he also spoke English fluently, and talked about this being a time of change. Some felt that his sympathies were divided, but he remained a respected figure in the community. Later, after he came through a thunderstorm alive when one of his companions was killed, he took the name Black Crow; the crow was the messenger of the thunder spirit.

Joe Healy had spent his life with horses. He was nearly seventy when Bobby Attachie showed up with Big Bird in the summer of '33. Joe liked the look of her. He liked her color. And he liked the way she moved. That was her Percheron blood, some said; and Joe knew that Percheron mares, like the stallions, pass on their qualities to their off-spring with remarkable consistency. The ranchers over at the Bar U had been bringing in Percherons for half a century, and had some of the best stock on the continent; but Joe could see that Big Bird had something special, even in that company. She was close coupled (you couldn't fit more than a hand's width between her last rib and the point of her hip) and had a deep girth, was well let-down (the lower part of her hind legs were shorter than the upper parts) and didn't show too much daylight (the legs were relatively short), had open elbows (you could fit your fist between the elbow and the rib cage), she stood over a lot of ground (her legs were square at each corner rather than bunched up underneath), there was plenty in front (well-proportioned neck and shoulders) and she had a bit of the dish-face of the Arab. Joe knew she was in foal, always a risk but a good one in her case because he could see she was a good keeper, in fine condition after that last winter. He could also see that Bobby knew how to look after horses.

For his part, Bobby didn't even try the tricks that traders have been using for thousands of years to hide a horse's faults—not letting her stand still, or not moving her much, keeping her close to the fence or far away from it. There's no such thing as a perfect horse, which means there are always things to find fault with; and he knew Joe would find them all.

Joe played his part and pointed them out. He came up with a long list. Then he looked in her mouth. "She's got some years; and she's got some more," was all he said. You can tell the age of a horse by the wear on the cups of the teeth (which disappear into a "dental star" by the age of nine), their shape, and the yellow-brown grooves at the gum line (which appear at about age ten and disappear when a horse approaches thirty), though some unscrupulous horse traders file the teeth and drill or burn the cups to fool a buyer. It's called "bishoping," after a Mr. Bishop—or maybe he *was* a bishop—who first tried it centuries ago. It's like changing the odometer on a car. Horses can live long, occasionally into their fifties and—so some say—even their sixties, depending on the breed, though thirty-something years is a good age; but even that leaves lots of time to try to fool someone.

Bobby hadn't ever tried; it wouldn't have worked with Joe anyway. Joe had gotten the truth straight from the horse's mouth. That's why you should never look a gift horse in the mouth; it's rude to check on the age of a horse that's been given to you.

But this was no gift horse, and after all that, Joe showed no interest. Bobby didn't argue with Joe's long list of Big Bird's faults. No point. Everything Joe said was true, and nothing he said mattered if he liked the horse. He didn't seem to. So Bobby said he didn't really want to sell her anyway. "She's the best horse we've ever had up there by the Peace," he added, unwilling to let Joe have the last word on Big Bird. Joe thought of saying something, but he didn't.

The deal apparently off, Bobby offered Joe some tobacco, and they smoked together, and had some tea, and talked about the weather, and baseball, and the Calgary Stampede, and the automobile safari with five Citroën half-tracks through the Peace River country to Alaska that Charles Bedaux had begun back in July. The summer had been wet, and the Citroëns quickly bogged down. By August—after staging a spectacular film scene in which two of the vehicles were driven over a precipice and another sunk in the rapids of a river—Bedaux and his party got on horseback. Bobby and Joe agreed that they should have started out that way.

Finally, Bobby got up to leave. Outside Joe's house, someone quietly had brought four horses and tied them up to the rail near Bobby's truck. None of them were great prizes, but all of them were good stock. And one was an Appaloosa, with a spotted coat that Bobby really liked. The Appaloosas had been bred by the Nez Perce along the banks of the Palouse River in what is now Washington.

"I'll take the mare for those four," said Joe. Bobby kept quiet. He knew horses, and had traded them for many years. But he also knew that he was playing with a big-leaguer here. He wasn't even born when Joe Healy had followed the last buffalo herd into Montana in the early 1880s.

So Bobby tried to wait it out. "Let's have a look," he said. A young lad came out of nowhere and walked them by, then ran them back. Bobby went over, looked at each carefully from about six feet away, watching the eyes and ears, the signs of splints and side bones, bog spavins, capped hocks and curbs, and then picked up the feet, checking for cracks in the walls and contraction of the heels, tapping the soles to see that they would take a shoe, watched breathing at the flanks for heaves, felt at the top of the heads for poll-evil, looked at the angles of the hoof and the pastern, ran his hand up each leg to confirm that the small problems he had seen from a distance—three of them had splints on the front cannon bone, one had a capped hock—were indeed small, and covered their eyes with his hands for a couple of minutes to check for moonblindness.

"I don't think so," he said, thinking so. "Big Bird's too good, and who knows how good the foal is going to be. Might just make my reputation." Joe turned and pulled a beautiful beaded canvas crupper (to keep a saddle from sliding forward) and a leather breast stall (to keep it from sliding back) from a pile in the corner on top of the old washing machine. The deal was done.

Big Bird wasn't paying any attention. She knew the drill. And anyway, she was busy, carefully positioning her lips around the purple flower of a big Canada thistle that was growing over by the pole barn in Joe Healy's yard. It was the perfect time of year for thistles.

Eating a thistle took time, and care. You had to separate the sharp leaves that protected the flower, flaring your lips to take the flack while sliding your tickly nose slowly past the prickles towards the most delicious flower in the whole wide world. Not every horse could do it as well as Big Bird. She had seen other horses watching her, trying to figure out how she got the thistle without once pulling back and snorting to clear all the confusion that the prickles had caused in her big nose, and then having to start again from the beginning. Now she was there; and as her lips closed around the flower, she heard Bobby calling her. Whoop, in it went, like a candy.

As she walked over to where Bobby and Joe were standing, she thought back to the spring. She had lost a lot of friends during the horrible winter, and even two of her foals from several years before had died. But the horses that made it through knew that summer would come like a gift of grace, everything blooming and growing for another year, flowers and fresh grass, sparkling water and sumac here on the prairies, and trees like the tamarack that would change color in the fall and become a golden promise of yet another spring.

When Big Bird's foal was born late the following spring, he was so pretty that one of the women began weaving a blanket for him right away. They called him Little Bird.

He had a slight overbite that made him look surprised all the time; but surprise was fine. In the way of poets and praise singers as well as those who are prey to others, he was always watching.

He moved like a dancer, but a country dancer rather than one of those dancers for the courts of Europe who have all the fancy moves. He liked line dancing and square dancing and circling round the sun. He ambled along in a lazy trot that he could keep up all day, enjoying the wonder of that moment—actually, it was no more than a split second—when all his four feet were off the ground and he was in the air, flying. Amazing Grace. Nobody seemed

The pure joy of running

to notice except Big Bird. And Joe Healy, who died two
years later, after watching Little Bird's first season on the
plains. The Creek poet Joy Harjo, famous for a poem titled
"She Had Some Horses," once wrote about the line
between the secular and the sacred being thin as a fishing
line. So is the line between the land and the sky where
horses come into their own.

Out on the grasslands by the Milk River ridge, where
humans had once hunted horses and where you could see
rivers running south to the Gulf of Mexico and north to
Hudson Bay, Big Bird's foal ran free. He ran on behalf of
Bobby Attachie and those Navajo horses and that little girl
who first rode a horse out on the steppes. He ran for the
horses of the Prophet and the chiefs of the Blackfoot and

the artists of all times, praising God and iiniiksi, the buffalo, and takh, the spirit horse of Mongolia, his ancient lineage. He was a covenant of wonder with the world, and as he ran he thought of how his Percheron forebears had broken the sod and brought the timber from the hills to build the houses and pulled the wagons that brought the families into town on Saturdays, and the Andalusians who had been the first to perfect the "noble gait," showing their glory in the schools of the Old World. And he thought of Midnight, the greatest bucking bronco of all time, born by that same Milk River, who terrorized the plains for fifteen years, piling the best riders high, wide, and handsome, and finally retiring, just last year, 1933, with a big celebration in his honor in Cheyenne, Wyoming.

And Little Bird thought of the great wild herds of the Altai Mountains and the Gobi desert, of the brumbies running up by the Gulf of Carpentaria and the mustangs in the Chilcotins, of the ponies of the northern moors of Europe and the southern cape of Africa. And he ran and ran and ran. Then he came back to Big Bird and the other mares bunched down in the coulee by the cottonwood trees, and nuzzled in. Home again.

NOTES AND ACKNOWLEDGMENTS

Telling tales about horses is an old habit, especially among fellow travelers. A few friends come first: Dix Anderson, Ted Zinkan, Bettie Vajda, Fred Hunt, Jim Hegan, Camille Joseph and Bill DuBois in the Kootenays, Tommy Walker in Spatsizi, Curlie and James Lindsell in Hertfordshire, and particularly John Burns at Bow Valley Farm, none of whom had any idea what mischief they were making when they gave me a leg up; Dorik Mechau, Carolyn Servid, John Straley, Gary Holthaus, Teresa Jordan, Sander Gilman, Neil Sterritt, David Chrislip, Carol Wilson, Peter Usher, Britt Ellis, Patrick Saul, George and Dianne Laforme, Derek Hopkins, Eddie Baugh, Elaine Melbourne, Janet Irving, Ramsay Derry, Rob Finley and John O'Brian, for encouragement; my sister Liz Food, for letting me work up some family stories; Richard Landon, for his knowledge of books; Paddy Stewart, for Pokey; Ian MacRae, for notes from the field; and Suha Kudsieh, for translations from Arabic.

Jan-Erik Guerth has been with me from start to finish as tamer and trainer, publisher and editor. I wouldn't have written this book without him. John Jennings has given me the benefit of his extraordinary knowledge and experience with a generosity of spirit which rivals that of the horses he knows so well. Without him, I *couldn't* have written this book.

Lorna Goodison has brought grace into my life and work, and I am forever grateful. And Geoff and Meg and Sarah made it all happen—watching, whispering, dodging hoofs, and asking me how the book was coming along with just the right mix of comedy and concern.

This book is dedicated to Reg Greer, at home in the Mulmur Hills.

And then there are all those whose writings have been indispensable, and whom I acknowledge in the notes that follow. I hope I also give a sense of a much wider literature, both as democratic and as aristocratic as any in the history of human civilizations.

In *Chapter One*, the memoranda from Mindy Christiansen and Harold McGill are slightly modified versions of documents in the archives of the Glenbow Museum in Calgary, Alberta. They were included in a brief prepared by me for a land rights case (*Apsassin*) that went to the Supreme Court of Canada in the 1990s, and was decided in favor of the Indians. The Meriam Report was titled *The Problem of Indian Administration* (1928); and Reeseman Fryer's description of the trauma of sheep units among the Navajo is from an unpublished monograph kindly made available to me by his daughter, Ann Van Fossen.

Information about colic is widely available . . . as is misinformation! I took some helpful details from M. E. Ensminger, *Horses and Horsemanship* (1969);

from Desmond Morris, *Horsewatching* (1988); from *Horse Conformation* (2004), edited by Juliet Hedge and Don Wagoner (in which there is a wealth of other information about horses on which I have relied throughout this book); and sometimes from grim experience. The anecdote about Percherons and the Paris Omnibus Company is from Y. Arthus-Bertrand and J.-L. Gouraud's *Horses* (2004); about the Kladruber and the Lusitano from Susan McBane and Helen Douglas-Cooper's *Horse Facts* (1990).

Information about the Blackfoot is from *Nitsitapiisinni: The Story of the Blackfoot People* (2001), published by the Glenbow Museum and put together by the (mostly) Blackfoot Committee that designed a permanent gallery there; from Frank G. Roe's *The Indian and the Horse* (1955) and John C. Ewer's classic *The Horse in Blackfoot Indian Culture* (1955), where the myth of the mallard (originally told by Head Carrier to Chewing Black Bones) is transcribed; from Hugh A. Dempsey's *A Blackfoot Winter Count* (1972); and from Blackfoot and other friends from the foothills. I am especially grateful to Frank Weasel Head for a conversation with me about Crop Eared Wolf (recorded by Kate McAll for a BBC broadcast in 2002).

Some of the stories about Kazaks throughout the book come from a chapter by Victor Shnirelman, Sandra L. Olsen, and Patricia Rice in *Horses Through Time* (2003), edited by Sandra L. Olsen, which also has some of the latest conclusions about the ancestry and domestication of horses (in chapters by Richard C. Hulbert, Jr. and David W. Anthony), on horses in history (by Juliet Clutton-Brock), and on the relatives of the horse (by Susan L. Woodward). It is a wonderful resource. My account of the evolution of equus also draws on George Gaylord Simpson's *Horses* (1961). Virginia Woolf's remark is from a lecture she gave in 1924, "Mr. Bennett and Mrs. Brown."

In *Chapter Two*, the description of the paintings in the Chauvet cave is from Jean-Marie Chauvet, Eliette Brunel Deschamps, and Christian Hillaire's *Dawn of Art: The Chauvet Cave* (1996). Jeff Opland was told "imbongi means eyes" by one of the greatest contemporary !Xhosa praise singers, David Manisi. Marshall McLuhan made his comment in *The Gutenberg Galaxy* (1962). The comment about "the Cadillac of colors" is by Maurice Telleen, in *The Draft Horse Primer* (1977), a book full of useful information. The best discussion of horse color is Ben K. Green's *The Color of Horses: The Scientific and Authoritative Identification of the Color of the Horse* (2001). The story of Jim Key is told by Mim Eichler Rivas in *Beautiful Jim Key: The Lost History of a Horse and a Man Who Changed the World* (2005), from which I also took the story about Alice Roosevelt. Among the many contemporary writers I mention Margaret Cabell Self, *The Horseman's Encyclopedia* (1963); Tom Dorrance, *True Unity: Willing*

Communication Between Horse and Human (1987); Ray Hunt, Think Harmony With Horses (1990); Vicki Hearne, Adam's Task: Calling Animals by Name (1986); Monty Roberts, The Man Who Listens to Horses (1996); Buck Brannaman, The Faraway Horses: The Adventures and Wisdom of One of America's Most Renowned Horsemen (2001).

My description of early hunting and herding benefited from Peter L. Storck's Journey to the Ice Age: Discovering an Ancient World (2004) and from (with specific reference to the Canadian prairies) Archaeology on the Edge: New Perspectives from the Northern Plains, edited by Brian Kooyman and Jane Kelley (2004), as well as from books on wild herds such as Hope Ryden's America's Last Wild Horses (1990), Martin Harbury's The Last of the Wild Horses (2004), and Monty Roberts's Shy Boy: The Horse That Came in from the Wild (1999). Wild About Horses (1998), by Lawrence Scanlan, is not primarily about wild horses, but gathers together some interesting material. For a good selection of horse stories, fact and fiction, Steven D. Price's collections of Classic Horse Stories (2002) and The Greatest Horse Stories Ever Told (2004) are hard to beat, along with regional reminiscences (and every region has them) and family histories such as MacEwan's Memory Meadows: Timeless Horse Stories (1997) and Teresa Jordan's marvelous Riding the White Horse Home (1993), and epic adventures like (though there is nothing quite like) Tschiffely's Ride: Ten Thousand Miles in the Saddle from Southern Cross to Pole Star, by A. F. Tschiffely (1933). On breeding, especially related to race horses, Kevin Conley's Stud: Adventures in Breeding (2002) is entertaining and informative, as is John Jeremiah Sullivan's Blood Horses (2004).

For Chapter Three, Sigurdur A. Magnusson's Stallion of the North: The Unique Story of the Icelandic Horse (1978) provided helpful information; and Morgan Baillargeon and Leslie Tepper's Legends of Our Times: Native Cowboy Life (1998) supplied many useful details, especially about events such as the first Calgary Stampede in 1912. The comment by Nez Perce Chief Joseph was published in the North American Review. The court case referred to is known as Delgamuukw, and involved the Gitksan and Wet'suwet'en Indians. They lost at trial and won on appeal.

The list of coaches is taken from Luigi Gianoli's Horses and Horsemanship Throughout the Ages (1969), an authoritative book from which I have learned a great deal. My discussion of pulling and pushing draws on The New Book of Saddlery and Tack, edited by Carolyn Henderson (2002), as does my account of saddles and stirrups and bridles and bits. A couple of details here and later are taken from Jean Deloche's Horses and Riding Equipment in Indian Art (1990). The comments by John Jennings are from personal correspondence and many conversations. The description of the horse tamer is by the rancher Fred Ing, and is quoted in Richard W. Slatta's *Cowboys of the Americas* (1990), along with other details about cowboy horse cultures.

In *Chapter Four*, John Keegan's comment about the Battle of Megiddo is from *The History of Warfare* (1993). Some of my commentary about the civilized and the barbaric is shaped by my disagreement with William H. McNeill's *The Rise of the West: A History of the Human Community* (1963). The passage from Isaiah is Chapter 31, verse 1. The challenge to the standard account of chariot charges is taken from Ann Hyland's *The Horse in the Ancient World* (2003), to which I am much indebted. My brief mention of packs and rigging doesn't indicate how much I have learned from Joe Back's *Horses, Hitches and Rocky Trails* (1959). General Eugene Daumas's cut-to-the-chase definition of the "horse of the orient" comes from *The Horses of the Sahara*, trans. Sheila M. Ohlendorf (1968), to which I turned for some commentary on Arab horses. The quotations about horses on the pampas and the plains are from a chapter by Deb Bennett and Robert S. Hoffmann on "Ranching in the New World" in *Seeds of Change*, edited by Herman J. Viola and Carolyn Margolis (1991).

For George Stubbs, I just stood there—as he had—looking at Whistlejacket, though in my case it was in the National Gallery in London. I also consulted Venetia Morrison's *The Art of George Stubbs* (2002), as well as the exhibition catalogue by Malcolm Warner and Robin Blake, *Stubbs and the Horse* (2004). John Baskett, *The Horse in Art* (1980) was a valuable resource on that general topic, as were T. K. Biswas, *Horse in Early Indian Art* (1987); S. D. Markman, *The Horse in Greek Art* (1943); Walter Liedtke, *The Royal Horse and Rider: Painting, Sculpture and Horsemanship 1500–1800* (1989); and Graham Budd, *Racing Art and Memorabilia: A Celebration of the Turf* (1997).

In *Chapter Five*, details of some of the games are from Monique and Hans D. Dossenbach's *The Noble Horse* (1987). Vladimir S. Littauer's *Commonsense Horsemanship* (1972) provided insights into the physics of jumping; and in the discussion of Caprilli's influence, once again John Jennings helped me out.

In *Chapter Six*, the comment about Galen is from Paul Veyne's *Did The Greeks Believe in Their Myths?* trans. Paula Wissing (1988); Herbert Simon's parable is from *The Sciences of the Artificial* (1969); and Joy Harjo's line from "Fishing" (*The Woman Who Fell from the Sky* [1994]). Some of Joe Healy's background comes from Hugh A. Dempsey's *The Amazing Death of Calf Shirt and Other Blackfoot Stories* (1994). Some I imagined, as I have imagined Bobby Attachie.

INDEX

INDEX

HORSE

HORSE

INDEX